Happy Memories

Chris Jesty

2QT Limited Publishing

First Edition published 2018
by 2QT Limited (Publishing)
Settle, North Yorkshire BD24 9RH United Kingdom

Cover Design by Dale Rennard

Printed in Great Britain by IngramSparks UK Ltd

A CIP catalogue record for this book is available
from the British Library ISBN 978-1-912014-10-1

Contents

Photographs

Introduction

In 2007 Martin Wainwright wrote of me 'One day his story will deserve to be fully told.' I have been writing that story, in the form of a diary, for over sixty years, and I have always hoped that one day it would be turned into a book.

People who know me may wonder why there is no mention in this book of some of the people and events that have played an important part in my life. The reason is that I didn't think that these would interest people who don't know me. On the other hand there has been no distortion of the facts to make the account more interesting.

The title was chosen to show that I have concentrated on events that I think people will enjoy reading about, although I may not have enjoyed all of them at the time.

Chapter 1

Origins

One day in 1936, Kenneth Wing Jesty and Hetty Irene Burr decided to get married and raise a family. So far as I am concerned, not only was that the best decision they made in their lives, it was the best decision that anyone has ever made in the history of the world – although I suppose that similar decisions made by my four grandparents, eight great-grandparents and so on were equally important. In fact, the story can be traced back through the common ancestors of human beings and chimpanzees and the common ancestor of those ancestors and gorillas and so on through orang-utans, gibbons, monkeys, other mammals, reptiles, amphibians, fish, starfish, flatworms, jellyfish, sponges, fungi, green plants, seaweeds, slime moulds and microbes. Many kinds of animals, such as birds and insects, are not included in this list because they are on separate branches of the tree of life. I have read that the quarks and gluons that make up most of my body go back even further, and are known to have existed 10^{-35} of a second after the creation of the Universe.

I was born on the 21st of June 1942, three days after

Paul McCartney and two days before Martin Rees, in Haymead's Hospital, Bishop's Stortford, which is five miles south of Ugley and nine miles east of Nasty. But that's not the beginning of my story. I know that I learned to appreciate music before I was born because I have read about experiments in which people have compared the reactions of new-born babies to music that they had heard before they were born with music that they hadn't heard before.

In fact, my personality and my appearance had already been determined by the time I became a zygote in 1941. I was then about a tenth of a millimetre across, about the size of a grain of sand, and just big enough to be visible to the naked eye. Before that I was mostly an ovum. I was well into middle age when I discovered that I had been an ovum since 1911. At that time it was already determined that if I reached maturity I would become a human being, but it was not yet determined what sort of person I would become or even whether I would be male or female.

In 1994 I tried to work out the odds against my having been born. In the past 600 years I have had about a million ancestors. If the odds against two people meeting and deciding to have children are ten to one, then the odds against a million couples meeting are ten raised to the power of a million to one. I found it impossible to believe that I had had that amount of good luck before I was born when I have had good and bad luck in roughly equal quantities ever since. I came to the bizarre conclusion that my existence cannot be just luck:

it had to be inevitable. This is a philosophical point that turns science upside down and that, so far as I know, nobody else has ever thought of.

In fact, the odds against two people meeting are much greater than ten to one. My mother's family came from the Bishop's Stortford area; my father's family came from the Yeovil area. What is the likelihood that both families would move to Walthamstow and that my parents would both belong to the same tennis club?

Supposing that my existence is the only inevitable thing, then not only could I have been any one of the hundred billion people who have ever lived, but I could have been born into any conceivable type of universe. It might have been a universe that only lasted for a few seconds; it might have been a universe in which nothing existed except myself. It would still have been a miracle. So it is an even bigger miracle that I have lived for more than seventy years and been able to see and hear and find out about a universe that is enormously interesting and complex.

I could regard my own existence as luck and the nature of the universe as inevitable, or I could regard my existence as inevitable and the nature of the universe as luck; either way, I have been extremely lucky.

Supposing the day I was born my mother had had twins. One of those twins would have been me. The other would not have been me. Now suppose that she only had one child. It might have been me that was born and my twin that was not born, or it might have been my twin that was born and me that was not born. It is therefore possible that my mother could have given birth to a child who looked exactly like me and had my personality, but who still wasn't me. This lengthens the odds against my being born even further.

A question I sometimes ask myself is this: if I had never been born, would I have been someone else? This leads to another interesting question: what do I mean by 'I' in this context? The implication is that I have always existed and always will do, which is nonsense.

My father was born in 1906 and my mother in 1911. My brother Jonathan was born in 1938 and my sister Amanda in 1945. My sister worked at various times for the BBC, the Bank of England, the World Council of Churches, the World University Service, the World Health Organisation and the International Labour Organisation. My brother spent most of his working life in the insurance business. He must have been successful in his field, for he talked on the subject on Radio London and on *You and Yours* on Radio 4. My father was the accountant, chief accountant or director of accounts of the British Council for thirty-three years, and he did his job so well he was awarded the MBE. He told me that he could have been the accountant for the National Trust, but they only offered him five pounds a week, whereas the British Council offered him five guineas a week. My brother-in-law Roger spent most of his working life in the United Nations. When I first met him in 1966 he was the editor of the magazine *WUS in Action*, which had a circulation of 10,000. When I met him again in

2014 he was the president of an association of former United Nations employees with 20,000 members.

I acquired the name Christopher from a friend of the family who died at about the time I was born. We inherited from him a leather suitcase that remained in the family until 1993, when it was left out in the rain and ruined. The name was first shortened to Chris when I started going to the Scouts in 1956. When I was very young my brother called me 'Fer', which was short for Christopher, then 'Ferman' and 'Freddie Ferman' and 'Finkle Fuffer Freddie Ferman'. Then it was shortened to 'Finkle Fuffer' and 'Finkle' and finally to 'Tink'. When I worked for Abacus Taxis in 1990 we used our Christian names as call signs, but as there were four drivers called Chris I was told that I would have to be Lionel. I couldn't imagine myself as a Lionel, so I said that I would be 'Tink'. I then became known to the other drivers by that name. I later came across the name Finkle Fuffer in the credits of a film and concluded that that was where it came from.

Chapter 2

Whistlefield

Of the first two years of my life I remember nothing. This is a pity because it was a very interesting period. I should have made a point of remembering it all so that I could tell people about it as soon as I learned to talk, but the idea of remembering never crossed my mind.

There must have been a time when it gradually dawned on me that the universe was very much larger than my own body. Lying in my pram, I would have noticed that when the pram was still the scenery was still and when I experienced a jolting the scenery moved. Just as the early astronomers couldn't tell whether the Earth or the stars were moving, so I couldn't tell whether my pram or the surrounding scenery was moving.

Like everyone else, I must have made the discovery at some time that the things I could see continued to exist when I could no longer see them. Nowadays I take this for granted, yet when I first used a word processor I thought that if the text disappeared from the screen it was lost for ever. It seems to me that the experience of being a baby is not very different from that of being a grown-up.

Of the following years I remember a great deal. I

remember knowing how old I was: I was three. There came a time when people tried to tell me that I was four, but I knew better. I also knew that all babies were girls and that all toddlers were boys. This means that I can remember the time when I didn't know that I had been a baby.

My earliest datable memory is of staying with my aunt at Rileys, a house in Sawbridgeworth on the London road, and of listening to the traffic on the road outside. I later learned that this was at the time my sister was born, which means that I was two years and ten months old.

I remember knowing that my father was thirty-nine and that my grandmother was seventy-nine. Then my father tried to tell me that he was forty and that my grandmother was eighty. I didn't believe this, so he explained it to me. He said that it must be true because 'twice forty is eighty'. I couldn't understand the logic of this, and I still can't. My father was born in November 1906, so this must have happened about six months after my fourth birthday.

For the first eight years of my life I lived in a beautiful thatched cottage called Whistlefield in Bedlar's Green, a quarter of a mile from Hatfield Forest. The living room was open to the roof and overlooked by a small room called the gallery, which was reached by a box staircase. This was where I had my office and this was where I did all my writing and drawing. The most notable thing about my output at that time was that it was not very good. I remember once writing: 'I've got Four Legs, Biggy, Leggy and Jump.' Then I realised that nobody

11

could tell from the sentence what I was talking about, so I added a second sentence: 'These frogs are frogs.'

I was always going to build a place called Secretland. It was all underground and consisted of a number of chambers linked by tunnels. The most important of the chambers was called the Perishamada. I hadn't learned to write, so I got my brother to write about it for me. Eventually I got round to building it. I got out the trowel and started to dig. When the hole was about a foot square and a foot deep, I realised that I had bitten off more than I could chew. I don't remember that Secretland was inspired by the underground home of the badger in *The Wind in the Willows*, but I think that it must have been.

I wanted to know what the highest number was. I decided that it must begin with 'nine hundred and ninety-nine thousand, nine hundred and ninety-nine million...', continue through billions, trillions and zillions, and end with '...nine hundred and ninety-nine thousand, nine hundred and ninety-*nine*.' Nowadays I would call it '$10^{96}-1$'.

I remember compiling a list of numbers that can't be exactly divided by other numbers. I started with the odd numbers, taking out 9, 15, etc., leaving 1, 3, 5, 7, 11 and so on, which I called indivisibilities. Later I learned that they were called prime numbers and that they should have started 2, 3, 5, etc. The question of whether '1' should be included is a matter of opinion and I don't think that I was wrong to include it, but the omission of '2' was clearly a mistake on my part. However, I would rather that I worked it out for myself and got it wrong than that

I learned about it and got it right.

The member of my family that I liked best was my brother Jonathan. Interestingly the person that I liked third best was myself. In later life I often thought that I liked some people better than others, but I never thought to compare other people with myself in this way.

Of my relatives, the one I liked best was my cousin Robin, who always signed his letters with his middle name Nigel. He is the only person I know with two Christian names, both of which are legitimate car registration numbers. I have always thought that if I could choose my registration number it would be CHR 1S, and I have actually seen the car numbered DAV 1D. Other interesting registration numbers that I have seen are 100 MPH, RUN 1N, TRY 1T, WE 2, 1 F, 1 AAA, ONE 23, 123 AB, 789 TEN, 22 TO, SAD IE, D1 CKY, D1 NKY, F1 SHY, SNA 1L, CAB 1N, S1 GHT, L1 NKS, M1 CAR, SET 1 and 1 AM. The last number could be a statement or a time of day, or it could refer to a member of the Institute of Advanced Motorists.

I remember that sport was dominated by Stanley Matthews (football), Denis Compton (cricket), Randolph Turpin (boxing), Stirling Moss (motor racing), Geoff Duke (motor cycling), Reg Harris (cycling) and Lester Piggott (horse racing). Most of them faded from prominence within a few years, but Lester Piggott kept on going through the 1950s, 60s, 70s, 80s and 90s.

I used to enjoy making models with plasticine and building houses with Lott's bricks and later Minibrix. Lott's Bricks were made of stone and Minibrix were made of rubber. The latter had the advantage that they couldn't be accidentally knocked down, but creativity was limited because the roofs came in fixed sizes.

We had a black-and-white cat called Soda. Sometimes he would be 'hibobbaresa' and rush around all over the place. I don't guarantee the spelling.

Once I was frightened by an owl, which I saw from the kitchen window, and I used to get nightmares about an animal called the Owl-dog.

I liked animal stories like *The Wind in the Willows*, but I thought that the animals should be portrayed behaving like animals and not like people. Then I found a book by someone called Rutley in which animals were portrayed in this way, but I lost it. If ever I asked people about it they would say, 'You mean Alison Uttley,' and I would say, 'Not Uttley, Rutley.' Sixty years later I found a couple of very small books by Cecily Rutley in a shop window in Kendal. The animals in it spoke English, but in all other respects they behaved like animals, just as I remembered them all those years before.

When I was very young, I used to frequently imagine myself being high up inside a large building like a warehouse. There was a particular feeling associated with this recollection that I have never experienced in any other circumstances.

If ever my mother sent a parcel, she would tie it up with string and seal the string with sealing wax. If she was particularly impressed by something she would say, 'By Jove.' I haven't heard this expression used for a very long time.

Scrapbook

From time to time my father would bring things home for me from the office. The best of these was a scrapbook. It had previously been used by the British Council and had become redundant when a new version was produced. The original material was still there, but there was plenty of space left for my own additions.

On the inside cover are the words:

CHRISTOPHER JESTY

SCRAP BOOK

AGE 6

The first two Ss and the J are back-to-front. Among the contents are:

1. Long printed words and printed words with two or more Cs in them. C was the first letter I learned because it was the first letter of my name. I no longer look on C as a special letter, but I still count the letters if ever I come across an exceptionally long word.
2. Photographs cut out of *The Times* (mainly from the autumn of 1948), including an aerial photograph of the Salisbury area.
3. Printed unicorns and lions.
4. My own drawings and paintings.

5. Pressed leaves of trees – oak, beech, ash, elm, lime, horse chestnut, hornbeam, maple, silver birch, hazel, pine, wild cherry, plum, guelder rose and sloe (actually spelt 'slow'). The horse-chestnut leaf was too big for the page, so I patiently waited until the following spring, when I could use a newly emerged leaf that was much smaller.

6. Cuttings from *The Children's Newspaper*, including twelve 'Countryside Flowers', nineteen photographs entitled 'Our Homeland' or 'This England', twelve Jacko and Chimp cartoons, twenty 'Bedtime Corners' and 'The Countryside in May' by the Hut Man.

There is also a book four-inches square made up of pieces of paper eight inches long, folded in half and stitched together with cotton. The reason it was stitched with cotton is that this was the only way I knew of acquiring a book with no printing in it. On each of the pages is a heading such as 'LONg Werds', 'A STORy', 'Pichers', 'NAMe', 'things I have' and 'PATANS CALAings'. On one page I wrote 'STICK things in here'. Then I realised that I hadn't left enough room for all the things I wanted to stick in there, so I added 'ONLee UNICORNANDLIONS'. By now, all the space I had left was four inches by two and too small for even one coat of arms. It was not until 2011 that I realised that this little book must have pre-dated my scrapbook, and it may have inspired my father to obtain one for me.

The garden

In front of the house and at the sides there were lawns and flower beds. At the back of the house there was an orchard. Behind that was a vegetable garden, and right at the back was a wilderness. My father used to remove weeds from the flower beds. I thought that this was a shame, and I decided that one day I would have a weed garden. Little did I know that we already had a weed garden – the wilderness – and that if we didn't remove the weeds the whole garden would become like it. One year the wilderness was transformed by the appearance of enormous daisies called marguerites, and I have a photograph of my sister surrounded by them.

When I climbed one of the trees in the orchard, I could see over the top of the house to the countryside beyond. This was my favourite spot in the garden, and I called it Landscape Corner. In amongst the golden rod there were a lot of little animals, and I called this area Natural Corner.

In the front lawn there was a swing and a sandpit; I used to enjoy making long tunnels in the sand with my arm and smoothing the entrances with my thumb. Close to the front gate was an apple tree with a hole in it at about the height of my head where snails used to shelter. I liked snails better than slugs because I could pick them up without getting slime on my fingers. One day it was decided that the tree should come down, and they made the cut above the snail-shell hole purely for my benefit.

Once I caught a lizard on the front lawn and its tail

came off in my hand. I felt very sorry for this poor lizard, but I later learned that they do this deliberately to prevent themselves from being caught. To see lizards, newts, frogs and toads was not unusual, but when I saw a grass snake in the garden it was a very special occasion.

School

From 1946 until 1950 I attended Miss Fitzmaurice's school, which consisted of one teacher and about ten pupils. I remember once someone at the school called me a human being. 'I'm not a human being,' I protested. 'I'm a person.' I also remember being shown a hornet. I have never seen one since.

In 1949 the school moved from Robert Corey's house in Hallingbury Street to Harps Farm, which was the home of one of the pupils, David Streeter. At this time my favourite song was 'The Teddy Bears' Picnic'. One day we all took our teddy bears to school. Among 'the family' were Dan (the cat), Ming (the panda), Wonk (the monkey) and Big (the large teddy bear). There was an identical teddy bear in the film *Words and Music*, which was released in 1948, and one like it was valued on the *Antiques Road Show* in 2013 at £4000. At Christmas 1949 I played the part of Prince Follidol in the school play. I have not been able to find this name on the Internet, and I wonder whether Miss Fitzmaurice wrote the play herself.

My favourite lessons were the weekly nature walks. On one of these walks I was overcome by the idea that from that moment onwards I was going to be absolutely perfect. I remembered seeing a boy flinging his raincoat over another boy's shoulders as a form of greeting, so I did the same to David.

'Ow,' said David.

'What's the matter, David?' asked Miss Fitzmaurice.

'Christopher hit me with his raincoat.'

'Why did you hit David with your raincoat?' demanded Miss Fitzmaurice.

They had played right into my hands. They had given me the chance to explain this wonderful thing that had just happened to me.

'I don't know,' I said.

In a way, that is the story of my life: beautiful ideas form in my mind, but when I try to turn them into reality they crumble into dust.

My best subject was reading, for which we used a series of books called the Beacon Readers. The item I liked best from these books was the poem that began: 'Little by little, an acorn said...' It was not until 2015 that I thought to search for it on the Internet. When I did so I found the first three verses very much as I remembered, but I had completely forgotten that the last two verses described my own ambitions and my subsequent efforts to bring them to fruition. One of the lines read: 'Whatever I do, I will do it well.' Unfortunately, people don't want things done well: they want them done quickly.

When I was seven years old there was a competition in which all the pupils were invited to write a composition about what they did in the school holiday. I won the competition in the same way that I won the competition to design a cover for the *Aberdeen University Motor Club Review*: I was the only contestant. My composition was never returned to me, but I remember two events that were mentioned. One was when I was walking with some friends and we found ourselves in Stansted Aerodrome. There was a man there working on an aeroplane, and he let us have a look inside the plane. The other was when I walked through Hatfield Forest to the hamlet of Bush End and back on my own. I listed the wild animals I had seen including fifty rabbits and two 'dears'. My mother thought that the 'dears' should have been called 'deer', but I thought that they should be called 'dears' because if they were the composition would be entirely my own work, whereas if they were called 'deer' I would have written every word except for one.

I have a photograph of my sister and myself in Whistlefield garden with three of our friends, Robert Corey, Angela Page and Vanessa Page. In 1995 my cousin Robin sent me a photograph showing two more friends, Mavis Lansdale and Susan, who was the granddaughter of the couple who ran the post office. In 1949 Alan and Susie Abrahams joined our school. They were the children of the athlete Harold Abrahams, who was later to be featured in the film *Chariots of Fire*. I don't have photographs of Alan and Suzie, but in 1998 I watched a television programme about their father that included photographs of Alan and Suzie taken at about the time

I knew them, and I was able to preserve their images on videotape.

When I left the school in 1950 my teacher wrote in my school report: 'Christopher is above all an "individual"; lazy; hardworking; tidy; untidy; alert; listless – according to his mood!' I have been like that all my life, but as I grew older the lazy periods became longer and longer until they accounted for 95% of my time, which is why this book has taken over three years to write.

The village

Adjoining our house to the north was an orchard where Old Man Howard had his caravan. The land has since been built on, as has the land adjoining our houses at Sawbridgeworth, Buckhurst Hill, Chigwell and Bridport. I remember once going to the Pages' house to see some puppets. For a long time the puppets lived in a world of their own: they talked to each other, but they never talked to anyone else. Then one of the puppets mentioned Mrs Page, and I wondered how the puppet knew her name. Nobody had told me that puppets were manipulated by people and that they had no minds of their own.

The couple who ran the post office were Mr and Mrs Alcock, who lived in the appropriately named house Oakside. When they retired they moved to a house in Orpington with the equally appropriate address of Commonside, Broomhill Common. Then the GPO decided to change the address to 44 Wiltshire Road, and

I thought that this was a terrible shame. Many years later, when I was working as a taxi driver in Southampton, I had to find a house in a road a mile long where every house had a name, and then I understood why it is better to give houses numbers rather than names.

I remember that in summer there were tar bubbles on the roads that could be 'popped' like the bladder wrack on the beach. In those days my favourite tree was the horse chestnut, because it had so many interesting features; now it is the oak, because it has been here much longer and supports more kinds of insect.

When I was very young an aeroplane crashed near our house and we brought back bits of metal called shrapnel. I often wonder if there is a record of this somewhere from which I could find out the date.

Travels

Twice a week there was a bus to Bishop's Stortford, once to get us there and once to bring us home again. We called it the Woolly Bus, presumably a corruption of 'village bus'. Otherwise we had to walk a mile to the Old Elm on the Roman road and get a bus from there. We used to get our food from Holland & Barrett's shop in Bishop's Stortford. I remember that there were little metal cylinders that flew around the shop above our heads like electric trains. I haven't seen these since we left the area in 1950. There is now a branch of Holland & Barrett's in Kendal, but I never go there because they don't sell the sort of food that I eat.

Sometimes, for a change, we would go to Dunmow where there was a pond with ducks on it. I found that the pond was still there when I revisited the area in 1986. At other times I would go into Stortford on the back of my mother's bicycle. On one occasion I made up a song as we went along and I called this my 'Long Long Song'.

I remember going to the seaside for the first time and discovering something I called 'wooshy-woo'. I was told that this was called sea water, and so it became 'wooshy-woo sea-waddy'. Sometimes when I came across a new word I would not get it quite right, so tractors became 'trackydons' and lorries became 'lollies'. Lorries with a load of hay were called 'hayhack lollies'. I still have this problem, but nowadays I can always write down the correct name.

The longest walk we did as a family was to Great Canfield, using the disused railway that is now known as the Flitch Way. I later worked out that we walked for fourteen miles. For me the highlight was studying ivy-covered trees looking for the thickest stems I could find. These still fascinate me, and in 2011 I found a tree near the Pennine Way where the trunk was completely covered in ivy stems.

The wealthiest people we knew were the Speechleys, with their daughters Valerie and Jennifer. They made their money from the manufacture of Christmas crackers. They lived in Warwick Road in Bishop's Stortford, and there was a table-tennis room in their attic. Leading off it were smaller rooms under the eaves, and this is where I acquired my love of attics.

We lived about thirty miles from London, which was then the largest city in the world. From time to time we would go there, taking the train from Bishop's Stortford to Liverpool Street. The last four stations, all within the built-up area of London, were inappropriately called Hackney Downs, London Fields, Cambridge Heath and Bethnal Green. The first time I went on the London Underground I was disappointed to find that the pictures were only in the stations and not all the way along the line, as I had been led to believe. In the stations we would sometimes pass the entrances to tunnels that we didn't go down, and I wondered where they all went.

I remember once going on a coach journey to Whipsnade Zoo. This time I was determined to memorise the route to find out where it was. I came to the conclusion that it was the other side of Hatfield Heath, which was completely wrong. The coach must have picked up some people in Bishop's Stortford and then some more people in Hatfield Heath and elsewhere before taking us all on to Whipsnade. Nevertheless the seed was sown: curiosity is the first step on the road to knowledge.

Of course, we also went to London Zoo. At one time I had seen all the animals I knew about except for the wolf. I think that if I had seen a wolf I would have been disappointed, because it is not all that different from an Alsatian dog. Three animals that I particularly wanted to see were the giant snail, the giant tortoise and the bullfrog because they were all larger versions of animals that were familiar to me.

I remember that the first time I went to Kew Gardens there were trees growing out of the roof of the palm house. If I could find out when the building was repaired, I might be able to work out how old I was at the time.

Yeovil

Sometimes we would travel all the way to Yeovil to visit my father's relatives. I used to enjoy walking round the town parks with my father. My favourite was Ninesprings, which consisted of a string of nine ponds each connected to the next by a waterfall. I remember going on a coach journey with my mother in the Yeovil area. Every so often there would be a beautiful view, but there was never enough time to study it. Then, at last, the coach stopped near one of these viewpoints and we were able to walk back to it. I expected the other passengers to do the same, but my mother and I were the only ones: all the others went into a public house. Much later I had the same problem while watching television, eventually solved by the invention of the 'pause' button.

On a later visit we went to Cheddar Gorge, and I have a photograph of myself high up on the side of the gorge. We also went to Weymouth, Wells and Weston-super-Mare but I don't remember much about these places.

Long ago I decided that, in the unlikely event that I was made a lord and had to decide where I would be lord *of,* I would choose Hatfield Forest.

Chapter 3

Sawbridgeworth

In 1950, my family moved to 14 The Forebury, Sawbridgeworth, and I started going to Harlow College. At Harlow College there weren't any nature walks, and my favourite subject was singing. Of all the songs we sang the one I liked best was 'The Ash Grove'. Many years later the song was played on the radio and I was able to add it to my collection, but they omitted the line 'In yonder green valley where streamlets meander' and replaced it with 'The friends of my childhood again are before me'. It was as though the song had been rewritten especially for my benefit.

At Harlow College there was a fives court, a building called the tectum and a tuck box in the playground where they sold sweets. I have never come across the word tectum since, and it's not in the dictionary. For dinner I used to have Welsh rarebit in the Cosy Café, where there was a map of East Anglia on the wall. Later I went home on the bus for dinner and I still had time to play reducing whist with my mother before I went back to school. I remember listening to an account of the King's funeral on the radio at school. The teacher said that this was something we would remember all our lives, but I thought that we would forget about it. My form mistress, Miss Scott, married a Mr Mathias, but I continued to call her Miss Scott. Once, when she said, 'What's my name?' I replied, 'Mrs Mathias, Miss Scott.'

When I was living in Sawbridgeworth I used to collect Victorian pennies. The bus conductors would save them for me; this way I obtained pennies for most of the years from 1860 to 1895. If I had two of the same date I would keep the one showing the most signs of wear. I later learned that most collectors do the opposite.

At the top of the Forebury on the right was a public hall where I once took part in a play. I don't remember what the play was about or my part in it. All I remember is that I had to go to Cubs with make-up on because there wasn't time to take it off. This was before I developed stage fright. It was in this public hall that I first heard one of my favourite songs, 'Over the Rainbow'.

Much Hadham

My brother and I used to explore the surrounding countryside by bicycle. The best place we discovered in this way was the village of Much Hadham, with its black-and-white Tudor houses, many of which bore dates. The oldest date was 1201. I went back there in 1957 and failed to find it, but I am sure that I didn't make a mistake. It is impossible that the house was as old as that, but the date may have recorded the fact that there had been a building on the site since that time. I asked my brother to photograph me outside some of these houses, and if you compare the resulting photographs with my illustrations in *East Anglian Town Trails* you will see how little my taste in architecture has changed over the years.

On the way to Much Hadham I remember seeing an enormous cross on the western horizon. It must have been on the ridge of high ground beyond Puckeridge. Much later I read that Henry Moore lived close to the route we took that day and that many of his sculptures were displayed in his front garden at the time. It is surprising that our parents didn't tell us about this. I wanted to know what lay beyond Much Hadham, and we eventually discovered the villages of Widford and Hunsdon, but if you look at a map you will see that they are actually no further away than Much Hadham. This was before I discovered maps.

'The Traveler'

In 1951, a few days before my ninth birthday, I wrote a poem called 'The Traveler' (so spelt). When I chose the title I didn't know that I shared a name with the patron saint of travellers, St Christopher. There are three verses of four lines each, and in each verse the second line rhymes with the fourth. There are no eye rhymes, and every line ends at a natural pause, which can't be said of some of the work of celebrated poets. I have kept the original to show that I haven't made any alterations to it since.

The only explanation I can find for my ability to write

this poem is that I was blessed with luck, followed by an enormous amount of luck, followed by the sort of luck that is needed to win a large amount of money on the football pools. I intended that the poem would be part of a book called *The River Rushes* and I tried to write a second poem, but by then my luck had run out.

On the facing page was a long drawn-out address including 'the world, the planet section, the Universe'. I used the phrase 'planet section' because I hadn't heard of the solar system. I also failed to mention that the solar system is in the Orion Spur of the Perseus Arm of the Milky Way, or that the Milky Way is in the Local Group in the Virgo Supercluster.

Here is the poem:

> The traveler goes for miles on end,
> Through country-side and towns,
> And sometimes for a day or two,
> Goes through some lonely downs.
>
> Through forests full of giant trees,
> With flowers here and there,
> He goes to lots of places,
> But nobody knows where.
>
> He sometimes stops at way side inns,
> And follows lanes and streams,
> Until his feet are tired and aching,
> Then sits and rests and dreams.

When I was older I would often go through those lines and think how well they describe the sort of life that I was later to lead, although I've stayed at very few wayside inns. I have stayed at more youth hostels, but 'youth hostels' wouldn't fit the rhythm of the poem, and I probably hadn't heard of them when I was eight years old. If I were to correct the poem the only changes I would make would be to respell traveller, countryside and wayside.

Our old black-and-white cat Soda died soon after we left Whistlefield and was replaced by a Siamese cat called So So. Then a dog called Shaggy Shenka joined the family. Cats are not blessed with the power of speech, but So So was able to express his feelings for the arrangement by his behaviour. This can be translated as: 'I am a very tolerant cat. I am prepared to allow a small number of well-behaved human beings in my house, but a dog, a *dog*, a *DOG*...! I will not have a dog in my house!' The dog had to go, and there has never been a dog in the household since.

It was in Sawbridgeworth that I first visited a public library. I particularly remember a big green book on natural history. Since then I have spent a lot of my time reading non-fiction books that I have borrowed from libraries, and I believe that I have learned more by doing this than ever I learned at school. Some of these books merely repeated things that I had read many times before, but others opened up a whole new subject for me. One of these was *Languages of the World*, which I discovered in 1991. Until I read this, I simply had no idea that there were so many languages or so many alphabets. Another book I discovered at around this time was *Butterflies of the World*, a collection of photographs of 5000 specimens from the Natural History Museum, all of them colourful, all of them beautiful. It would have taken a lifetime to study them and learn their Latin names.

The best book I have read about the English language is *The Language Instinct* by Stephen Pinker; the best book I have read about palaeontology is *Life: An Unauthorised Biography* by Richard Fortey; the best book I have read about taxonomy is *The Variety of Life* by Colin Tudge, and the best book I have read about mathematics is *The Penguin Dictionary of Curious and Interesting Numbers* by David Wells. The best books I have read about astronomy include *The Key to the Universe* by Nigel Calder, *Companion to the Cosmos* by John Gribbin and *Philip's Astronomy Dictionary*. My discovery of these books could not have taken place unless they had previously been discovered by the people who acquire them for the libraries. To such people I owe an enormous debt of gratitude.

My favourite works of fiction are the William books by Richmal Crompton, especially those published between 1924 (*William the Fourth*) and the end of the 1930s. I noticed that both A.A. Milne and Richmal Crompton displayed an ignorance of physics in their writing. In *The House at Pooh Corner*, Eeyore the donkey is washed to the bank of a stream by the waves from a dropped stone, but this wouldn't happen because the water in the waves moves up and down. Similarly, in one of the William books a snowman is given an overcoat, which causes it to melt. Overcoats keep people warm because we have an internal source of heat, and the overcoat prevents the heat from escaping. A snowman has no internal source of heat and would stay at the same temperature.

One of my favourite maps is the one-inch Ordnance Survey map of the North York Moors, which was published in 1966. Unlike other one-inch maps, it uses pale green for the lowlands and various shades of brown for the uplands. Another of my favourites is the Ordnance Survey physical map of Great Britain on two sheets, published in 1957, which shows only natural features. My favourite poem is *The Brook*, which was written by Alfred, Lord Tennyson in 1855. I learned it by heart a century later in 1955.

Chapter 4

Buckhurst Hill

In 1952 the family moved from Sawbridgeworth to 10 Stag Lane, Buckhurst Hill. Before doing so, we looked at a number of other houses, including one at Harlow that had a large cluster of outbuildings at the back, and I added a love of outbuildings to my love of attics.

10 Stag Lane was a yellow-brick, grey-slate, semi-detached house just like thousands of others. I was very disappointed with it, but it did have a redeeming feature: there was a cellar that could be reached from the garden or from the cupboard under the stairs, and from the cellar you could get into the foundations of the house. It was at this time that I added a love of cellars to my love of attics and outbuildings.

From our house it was a quarter of a mile walk via Tuttlebee Lane to Epping Forest, the same distance as from Whistlefield to Hatfield Forest. Discounting conifer plantations, there are very few forests in England, and I was remarkably lucky to live so close to two of them.

Stag Lane took its name from the Bald-faced Stag, the public house where the pianist Gladys Mills was discovered. From my bedroom window I had an unobstructed view across the suburbs of north London to Alexandra Palace, which was the BBC's main television transmitter at the time. There were several church steeples in the view, but I found that the number visible varied from day to day. It was at Buckhurst Hill that I first saw a television set. The Mynotts next door had one, and they invited us in to watch the coronation of Queen Elizabeth II. It was not until 1958 that we acquired one of our own.

At school we made a model of Westminster Abbey, where the coronation took place, each pupil being responsible for a particular part of the building. At the end of term I acquired some of the decorations, and I put them up in my bedroom.

When I was living at Buckhurst Hill I started to collect the labels from matchboxes that were lying at the side of the road. I found that the Epping New Road was a better source than the High Road because it led to more distant parts of the country. Altogether I collected ninety-one labels and I still have them. I could have had more if I had kept all the Clock Brand labels because each one showed a different time, but in the end I decided to keep only one.

Every year, around June 21st, I would have a birthday outing. In 1953 I wanted to go to Ivinghoe Beacon, which I had admired at a distance from Whipsnade Zoo, but it was decided that instead I would go with my mother to the stately home of Hatfield House. On the way there, between Potters Bar and Hatfield, we passed a number of tall poles on the right. Then I took a double take: one of the poles was much taller than the others and reached a prodigious height. I worked out that it should be visible from High Beach, and the next time I went there I found it. It occurred to me that it might even be visible from my bedroom window, and sure enough, by piling up the furniture I managed to see it. I gave it the name Hatfield Pole. Later on I learned that it was called the Brookmans Park Transmitting Station and that the height of the tallest mast was 500 feet.

I found Hatfield House a disappointment. We went round in a group of people, one of whom distracted our attention by talking all the time. One of the things I liked about Berkeley Castle was that you could wander around without a guide. Back in the town of Hatfield I overheard my mother enquiring about buses to Dunstable, and then I knew that we were going to Ivinghoe Beacon. Ivinghoe Beacon was not a disappointment. There was a strong breeze and there were cowslips everywhere, but what inspired me most was the wonderful view; I think that I must have been lucky enough to arrive on a very clear day. Ivinghoe Beacon was for me what Orrest Head was for Wainwright.

On 9th January 1954 I won a copy of *Tom Sawyer* in a children's essay competition about how to improve my junior library. On 1st January 1955 I went with my brother to see *This is Cinerama* at the London Casino, and I thought that I had never seen anything so beautiful before. In 2010 I saw it again at the National Media

Museum in Bradford. This was the only place in Britain where it could still be seen, and I was lucky that it was only sixty miles from where I was living at the time.

Daiglen

Soon after we moved to Buckhurst Hill I started going to Daiglen School in Palmerston Road. I remember running down the outside staircase and thinking that if a film were made of my childhood the film makers would have to find someone who could run downstairs quickly to play my part. Actually it was not totally impossible that a film would be made of my childhood because that is what happened to Gerald Durrell. Similarly, before I left for Wareham in 1958 I imagined myself singing about Dorset in front of a live audience. This was impossible because I couldn't sing, but something like that did happen to Bonny Sartin of the Yetties.

We used to play rugby on the banks of the Ching in Epping Forest, and a boy called Palmer was the only one who could jump across the stream.

Isle of Wight

In 1953 we had our first family holiday based at Freshwater Bay on the Isle of Wight. I remember going to Carisbrooke Castle and being disappointed to find that it was not properly ruined: though starting to crumble in places, the walls were largely intact. We also went to Tennyson Down, Alum Bay, Blackgang Chine

and St Boniface Down. The bus journey to Freshwater
Bay from the east with Tennyson Down in the distance
I always associate with a tune that I later learned was
the 'Prelude to Suite No 1' by Bizet. The highlight of the
holiday was flying round the island in an aeroplane with
my mother.

Swanage

The following year, my mother, my sister and I had a
holiday based at Swanage, and I discovered the beauties
of the Isle of Purbeck for the first time. It was this holiday
that inspired me to move to Dorset in 1958 and to
produce a book about the area in 1982. Among the places
we visited were Ballard Down, the cliff-top near Old
Harry, the village of Worth Matravers and Corfe Castle.
I was pleased to discover that, unlike Carisbrooke, Corfe
Castle was quite definitely ruined. I have a photograph
of myself on the top of an old wall that I later learned
was part of the Gloriette.

I remember seeing an enormous grasshopper in
Swanage and thinking that it must have come on a boat
from a foreign country and jumped ashore. I later learned
that it was a great green bush cricket and quite common
in the Swanage area.

Buckhurst Hill County High School

From 1953 until 1958 I attended Buckhurst Hill County
High School, which was situated midway between

Buckhurst Hill and Chigwell on the banks of the River Roding. In the first year I was in the A stream because I got a high score in the scholarship examination, but after that I was always in the lowest stream. My best subject, and the only subject that I thought was useful, was English language. I was helped in this by Mr Gray, who knew that I wanted to be an author and showed me how to construct sentences properly.

In 1953 I was taught chemistry for the first time. I learned about substances called chemicals with names like 'nitrogen' and 'sulphur', and what happened when you mixed one substance with another, but nobody told me what these chemicals *were*. I thought that they must be substances that people dug up out of the ground and that the reason people dug them up was to find out what happened when they were mixed together. If it had been explained to me that everything in the world is made of chemicals, and that chemical reactions are going on around us all the time, I am sure that I would have found the subject much more interesting than I did.

When I was at school I made a number of discoveries in the realm of mathematics, and I often wondered whether there were other discoveries still to be made. Many years later I learned about imaginary numbers, which are the square roots of negative numbers and neither negative nor positive. I thought that they could be of no possible use, but I later found out that there are equations that can only be solved using these numbers. Now I wonder what aspects of mathematics there are that I still don't know about and never will.

I left school with four 'O' level passes, English language (distinction), English literature, mathematics and geography.

The Bus Club

On 12th January 1954 I started a club made up of pupils of my own age, which I called the Bus Club. I have found references to twenty-one members in my diary and in surviving documents, but they were not all members at the same time. The club was inspired by the Outlaws in the William books by Richmal Crompton. One difference was that William's leadership was never challenged, whereas mine was. On one occasion it was proposed that a boy called Nutmeg should become the leader, and I was outvoted. I once wrote 'Leader Nutmeg, official leader Jesty' on a club document and Nutmeg objected, saying that I was not the official leader, but this was just my way of saying that it was still my club because I started it. Looking back, I am inclined to the view that he was right and I was wrong: I was not the official leader. But if I had written 'Leader Nutmeg, founder Jesty' and he had objected to that I would have been right and he would have been wrong. The moral of this tale is that it pays to have a good working vocabulary.

I also started up the Junior Natural History Society. We held meetings and showed films and arranged visits to the Natural History Museum, Kew Gardens and Whipsnade Zoo. At one time there were thirty-two members but, as with many societies, the number of active members was much smaller.

Papers relating to the Bus Club (later to be renamed the Ghost Club) and the JNHS went into my scrapbook. Among these papers are the *Ghost Club Magazine* of September 11th 1954, including a crossword, a maze, a map and an article entitled 'How Things Began', which can be summarised in one sentence: I had no idea how things began. I remained in ignorance of the origin of the Universe until I read an amazing account of it in 1979.

Astronomy

The first time I looked at the stars, I was disappointed to find that they were not arranged in constellations as I had been led to believe. In fact, if they had been arranged in constellations they would have been much less interesting because it would mean that they had been put there by people and were therefore not very far away. It was only when I moved to Buckhurst Hill in 1952 that I started to study them seriously. One day I noticed a lot of stars very close together, and I later learned that they were called the Pleiades. This was the first indication I had that the stars were not arranged completely at random. In later life I could only see six of them, but in those days my eyesight was much better and I could see thirteen. Apparently the record is seventeen, but the difference in brightness between the thirteenth and seventeenth is very small.

On the other hand, I read about the Milky Way

before I saw it for myself. In fact, I looked for it several times and failed to find it.

I have continued to be interested in astronomy ever since. I used to think that all the stars were the same distance away, but then I learned that some are farther than others. I thought it would be interesting to find a star that was easy to locate but was much further away than most of the other stars. Eventually I discovered Deneb, which is 2600 light years away at the end of the shortest arm of the Northern Cross. So, if anyone asks you what is the farthest place visible from Snowdon or Ben Nevis a good answer would be Deneb (or 'the Swan's tail').

Here are some more of my observations on astronomy. The Earth orbits the Sun at 67,000mph; the Sun orbits the centre of the Milky Way at 500,000mph, and the Milky Way is moving towards the constellation Serpens Caput at 1,300,000mph relative to the cosmic background radiation. So, if anyone asks you what is the maximum speed of a particular vehicle, a good answer would be 1,300,000mph.

It is generally thought that, apart from the Earth, there are six planets that are visible to the naked eye, but there is one more, Uranus, that can sometimes be seen by people with exceptionally good eyesight. There is a well-known song that begins: 'While shepherds watched their flocks by night...' Those words would never have been written if there hadn't been thousands of people engaged in a similar activity for hundreds of years. Apart from watching their flocks there wasn't much for these people to do except to study the stars. No doubt most of them concentrated on the brighter stars, but there must have been some who preferred to study a small area of sky. Surely a few of these would have noticed a very faint star that changed its position over time and must therefore be a planet. There could have been many arguments over the years between people who claimed that there were seven planets and people who thought that there were only six because they couldn't see the seventh and because 'everybody knows' that there are only six.

There are sun-like stars a thousand million years older than the Sun, which means that there may be civilisations millions of years in advance of ours. It is extremely unlikely, but not impossible, that one of them may discover the Earth in the near future and share with us their latest discoveries and inventions.

Chapter 5

Chigwell

I first started to write a diary in 1953 when I was ten years old, but I lost it. The first diary to survive opens on 25th December 1954, with a list of my Christmas presents followed by the announcement that my father had decided not to buy the lovely six-bedroomed house at Chingford that we had been to see. It looked straight across the golf course to Epping Forest; if we had bought it, I would have had my own office as I had had at Whistlefield.

Instead we moved to a brand-new house at 61 Chigwell Park Drive, Chigwell, which was part of a housing estate built by a firm of builders run by my uncle Arthur. My father also bought the adjoining land that would have been number 63, so that we had a large garden adjoining the countryside. The house was situated right on the edge of London: we could walk across the fields to the River Roding and follow the river upstream to the open country without passing through a built-up area; or we could go up the hill to Chigwell station, turn right to Ilford and turn right again to central London without passing through any countryside. When the boundaries of Greater London were fixed in 1965 they included the whole of the Metropolitan Police district except for Chigwell because it was thought that the people of Chigwell would rather be in Essex.

The position of the house was on the left bank of Chigwell Brook where it was joined by a smaller stream, which meant that there were streams running along two sides of our garden. A few days before we moved in, a friend of my sister told us that the smaller stream was called the Chig, but I have never found it referred to as such in the literature. Once I saw a woodlouse that appeared to have fallen into the stream and become squashed, but it was moving around quite happily. Then I saw another one exactly the same and realised that they must belong to a different species. In fact, they were freshwater shrimps. The most interesting creatures I found in the stream were entirely covered in tiny stones. I later learned that these were caddis-fly larvae.

When we moved in there were fences between the garden and the streams, but my father had them removed. We planted tiny oak and beech trees alongside the fence separating our garden from the one next door in the hope that they would become a hedge. The beeches were a success, but the oaks were not. The lawn at the side of the house was used for playing tennis. Most people would say that you need at least two people to play tennis, but we had a chalk line on the garage wall marking the top of the net, and this made it possible for one person to play.

There was an artificial pond in the garden into which we introduced goldfish, but frogs and newts found their own way there. Once I saw a spider in the garden with an egg sack that was beginning to hatch, and a lot of tiny white spiders crawled out. I later learned that this was a wolf spider.

Close to the confluence, the Chig passed through a narrow gap between a tree and the abutments of a bridge. Here I built a dam using the half-bricks that were abundant in the area and clay that was exposed in the banks of the stream. It seemed to take an enormous amount of time, but I could tell from the progress I was making that if I kept going long enough it would be finished. And so it was, and a small pond was created on the upstream side of the dam.

I also tried to build a tree house with the help of Tim Chowns. We had some luck at the beginning when an old door floated down the stream. The door, which was going to be the floor of the house, was reached by means of a rope ladder. We found it very difficult to find a level place in the tree, and it was even more difficult to get the door up there, but eventually we succeeded. That, however, was as far as the enterprise went; the impact that we made on the countryside was infinitesimal.

In the summer, when it wasn't muddy, I would sometimes walk to school across the fields using a tunnel under the railway that is no longer there. Once I found a grass snake and took it to school with me. Everyone was very interested.

We had two Siamese cats that had their own trap door so that they could go in and out of the house and explore the neighbouring fields, but if ever we tapped the walking stick to tell them that we were going for a walk they would come running from wherever they were to join us. This shows that animals don't only associate themselves with people because we provide them with food and shelter; they also do it for the company.

I used to enjoy drawing maps that showed rivers and streams but nothing else. If the valley of a river continued beyond the source I would show this on the map. The most remarkable example I found was the River Colne in Hertfordshire. On the Ordnance Survey one-inch map the blue line ends between Hatfield and St Albans, but the valley continues for a further fourteen miles through Sandridge, Nomansland Common and Harpenden to Zouches Farm near Dunstable.

Among the tunes I learned to play on the piano were 'Singing the Blues', 'Happy Days and Lonely Nights', 'There is a Tavern in the Town', the 'Bluebell Polka' and '*Que Sera Sera*'.

Scouts

My brother's friend Trevor was the assistant scoutmaster of a local Scout troop, and in October 1956 he invited me to join. My first camp was near Oxshott in Surrey in June 1957. Studying the Ordnance Survey map of the area I discovered that the campsite was within walking distance of Chessington Zoo, and I organised an expedition there.

In April 1958 I accompanied Ken Baker on his first class hike from Tunbridge Wells to Withyham, where we set up camp. The following day we joined other members of the troop at Broadstone Warren. The campsite consisted of about a square mile of forest and was by far the best site I have seen. Our route took us through Ashdown Forest, and I remember thinking how closely it resembled the forest of the Winnie-the-Pooh stories, but it wasn't until 1965 that I discovered that they were the same place.

The badge that most appealed to me was one for which I would have to travel to an area of mountains and write about them. I studied the maps and found that the nearest suitable area was the Black Mountains on the border of England and Wales. I was told that I couldn't do that badge, but that I could do the Master Cook badge, which didn't appeal to me at all. However, I wanted to get as many badges as I could, so I went on the Master Cook badge course weekend at Little Heath on 17th-18th May 1958. Of all the camping sites I have used this was the least interesting, consisting merely of a rectangle of grass in the outer London suburbs. I didn't do any cooking because the other Scouts did it all, but I still got the badge.

Travels

When I went to Ivinghoe Beacon in 1953 my mother did all the planning, but by 1956 I was planning bus journeys myself. I wrote to the London Transport Executive public relations officer for ten North London bus timetables and planned a journey to Whipsnade using two five-shilling and two half-crown Country

Bus Rover Tickets. We left Chigwell at 9.28am on 1st September 1956 and arrived at Whipsnade at 3.43pm, changing at Abridge, Epping, Hertford, Letchworth, Hitchin, Luton and Markyate.

The first time I stayed at a youth hostel was on 3rd–5th September 1956, when I went with my brother to Patcham Place near Brighton and walked along the ridge of the South Downs to Steyning.

From 31st December 1956 until 6th January 1957 I travelled round Surrey and Sussex with Trevor and four other Scouts, staying at the youth hostels of Holmbury St Mary, Blackboys and Patcham Place (again). The hostel I liked best was Blackboys, which was situated in a wood by a farm. While we were there we split up into three groups to produce maps of neighbouring villages. We returned to London in the luxury of the Brighton Belle.

When we were in Brighton I came upon a most extraordinary building that I later learned was the Brighton Pavilion. I had a similar experience later on when I was passing through the town of Fontainebleau near Paris and came upon the imposing entrance to a stately home. I later learned that the Palace of Fontainebleau was perhaps the most famous palace in France apart from Versailles.

It was in 1956 that I discovered hitch-hiking, which enabled me to travel to places that I couldn't possibly reach in any other way. The first time I did this on my own was on 20th January 1957, when I went from Chigwell to Finchingfield and back, passing through the Rodings, Great Dunmow and Great Bardfield. I chose

Finchingfield because I had never been there before and because it is reputed to be the most beautiful village in Essex. I look on this as one of the landmarks in my life, like my walk to Bush End in 1949 and my journey to Greece in 1963. In a way my journey to Morocco in 1995 was also a landmark because it was the first time I left Europe, but I actually got no further than I did in 1963.

When I was hitch-hiking I met some remarkable people. The most famous was Sir Vivian Fuchs, the director of the British Antarctic Survey. He was driving an E-type Jaguar from London to Cambridge, and we did 134mph, which was legal at the time. Other people I met in this way included Bertrand Russell's secretary (who features prominently in Russell's autobiography), the managing director of McAlpines (who was driving a Jaguar XJ12) and the songwriter Tony Hiller. I also met the only person in the country who makes nets for catching rabbits, a professional balloonist (one of only four in the country), the author of a book about caving, the author of a book about fish, someone who had written a television programme about Offa's Dyke Path, someone who had written about the Snowdon panorama in a local newspaper, and the parents of someone who had stayed in my cottage.

On 22–24th March 1957 I went on a school field weekend in the hills around Dorking. The tune that I always associate with this weekend is 'Lullaby of Birdland'. I later went to the Yorkshire and Derbyshire Dales and to Snowdonia with the school.

On 21st April 1958 I went on a school visit to

Cadbury's factory in Birmingham. When we got to Warwick the coach stopped and we walked round the town. One of our boys (whose name I shan't mention) removed the cap from the head of one of the local boys. Then I climbed up some scaffolding and placed the cap over the end of a pole that was jutting out. I don't know whether the boy ever got his cap back. We left Warwick without knowing that it contained a very large and famous castle. It is understandable that none of the boys had heard of it, but it is surprising that the teachers didn't mention it, just as it is surprising that my parents never mentioned Henry Moore when I went to Much Hadham. On the way home we sang a song that began 'Sweet violets, sweeter than the roses...' The song was very short, but I think of this as one of my happiest memories. I never heard the song again until it was played on the radio fifty years later.

Cornwall

On 9th August 1957 we set off in my father's Wolseley for Trevean Farm in West Cornwall. I helped out on the farm by feeding the chickens and milking the cows, which I found very difficult. I noted that stacks are made up of mows, which are made up of shocks, which are made up of sheafs.

We explored the whole area around Land's End and the Lizard peninsula. The places I liked best were the Logan Rock, Porthcurno Bay and St Ives. One evening we went to see *Twelfth Night* at the open-air theatre.

Other family holidays included Snowdonia (1955), Yugoslavia (1960), Ullapool (1962), Sark (1963) and Ireland (1965).

In 1957 I acquired an atlas of Great Britain at the scale of three miles to an inch, and I learned the whereabouts of most of the towns. I decided that the place where I would most like to live was the hamlet of Row in the remotest part of the Lake District. Since then I have never seen the hamlet referred to as anything but Wasdale Head. In 1974 I came to live within two miles of it.

Robert Robinson, the chairman of *Brain of Britain*, once said that he had never heard people using rhyming slang, but I have. At Buckhurst Hill County High School I heard people using the expressions 'use your loaf' meaning 'use your head', and 'let's have a butchers' meaning 'let's have a look'. It was only later that I learned that 'loaf' is derived from 'loaf of bread', which rhymes with 'head', and that 'butchers' is derived from 'butcher's hook', which rhymes with 'look'.

The prospect of leaving school and starting a new life was like travelling along a long tunnel with a light at the end of it: the light got closer very slowly and I felt as though I was never going to reach it, but eventually I did. I had a similar experience when I was approaching the time that I would leave Minicabs and buy my rally car, and again during the days before my arrival at the Snowdon Summit Hotel.

Chapter 6

Wareham

In 1958 I applied for a job with the Forestry Commission. They asked me which county I wanted to work in and I chose Dorset. Then they sent me to Wareham Forest. My first address was 39 Carey Road, Wareham, later to be renumbered 73. From my window I could see Ballard Down, Nine Barrow Down, Corfe Castle, Knowle Hill, Grange Arch, Flowers Barrow, Bindon Hill, Poole Harbour, the Arne peninsula, Poole power station and Wareham Mill. Many of these places were later to be featured in my guide to the Isle of Purbeck.

I was an apprentice, but I did the same work as everyone else. Whenever it rained we used to play cards, and I remember that I could tell which cards one of my opponents held by looking at the reflection in her glasses.

In the evenings and at weekends I explored the surrounding countryside. The farthest place I reached was Bath, where I visited the Roman baths and mineral springs. Whenever I had visited Roman remains previously all I found were foundations, but here the Roman walls rose to a considerable height and there were statues all round the site. Later I revisited the area and realised that the statues and the higher parts of the walls were all relatively modern.

On 7th October 1958 I went to a dancing class. The first instruction was to choose our partners. I went straight up to the prettiest girl in the room and asked if she would be my partner. To my absolute delight she agreed. So far, so good. The next instruction was to start dancing. I danced like a newborn calf walks: I did everything wrong. Eventually my partner said, 'I can't do this,' and ran out of the room. Later on, when I was at college, I went to another dancing class. The same thing happened, but this time my partner behaved quite differently. She went up to another couple and said, 'Will you change partners with me?' At this point I gave up the idea of learning to dance.

When I had been in Wareham for about five months my parents asked me whether I would like to return home and go to the South-West Essex Technical College in Walthamstow. As I always did when I had something to think about I walked round the town walls. It was arranged that I would phone my mother when I had made up my mind. This was our conversation: I said, 'I have decided what I want to do. I want to stay in Wareham.' My mother said, 'Are you sure?', and I said, 'No I'm not sure: I want to go to college.' As I spoke I knew that I would never regret it, and I never did. I don't claim that this is a good way of making decisions, but it worked on this occasion. I look on my college days as among the happiest of my life, and I have never felt so much a part of a community as I did while I was there.

Dreams

Over the years I have had many interesting dreams. The most remarkable thing about them is that I never decide what I am going to dream about. So who does decide?

On 2nd February 1957 I dreamed that I was exploring an old house.

On 15th March 1957 I dreamed that I rowed a boat from Sawbridgeworth to Roydon.

On 15th November 1958 I dreamed that I was on the first manned space rocket to the Moon, but I failed to reach it and came down after four hours.

On 23rd July 1959 I dreamed that I was made a police superintendent as a reward for removing a parked car that was holding up the traffic. I told lots of people what to do and rowed someone out to a liner because he had just missed it.

On 5th December 1959 I dreamed that I went to America, got married and bought a $370,000 house.

On 30th January 1960 I dreamed that we were on a rally, and that when we were halfway down Bournebridge Lane we remembered that we had left the car at Lambourne End.

On 8th December 1980 I dreamed that I caught a bus in the Lake District and they charged me £52, which I thought was rather expensive.

On 14th March 1995 I dreamed that I became a close friend of Cliff Richard.

On 28th November 1995 I dreamed that I met the Beatles. I had already met the Prince of Wales in a dream.

On 11th October 2002 I dreamed that the Queen was a passenger in my taxi. I had to take her to a railway station, but I didn't know the way.

On 9th November 2002 I dreamed that I explored an extremely large and extremely beautiful stately home.

On 6th January 2003 I dreamed that I got married. When I got to the wedding I realised that there should have been a best man.

On 28th November 2003 I dreamed that I met Hayley Mills, who had recently been on television.

On 25th October 2004 I dreamed that I was appointed Poet Laureate and that I owned a Rolls Royce.

On 16th November 2004 I dreamed that I could travel downhill by sitting down and floating along a few feet above the ground.

On 14th October 2005 I dreamed that I bought a dustpan, and it came with a book of instructions that was about an inch thick.

On 26th March 2010 I dreamed that I was in the square in Keswick and surrounded by ruined buildings, and I said to somebody 'I was here yesterday and it wasn't like this then.'

On 27th March 2010 I dreamed that the publishers changed all the hand lettering in the Wainwright books to typesetting, and I refused to work for them any more.

On 5th December 2011 I dreamed that I went back to Whistlefield, and that everything inside had been changed out of all recognition.

On 25th August 2014 I dreamed that I made an important scientific discovery and that I had to get to Manchester University to tell them about it, but I couldn't find the university.

When I am dreaming I believe that what I am dreaming is really happening to me. If I am capable of believing that something is really happening when it isn't, how can I be sure that what I believe is happening to me when I am awake is really happening?

Coincidences

Throughout my life I have experienced remarkable coincidences. For example, in 1960 I went to the village of High Beach to ask the landlord of the King's Oak if he could cater for the end of the Romer Rally. Unfortunately, there was no answer when I rang the bell. As I was about to leave someone asked me what I wanted and when I told him, he said he had come there for exactly the same purpose! When I applied to enter his rally he said that his name was almost exactly the same as mine – Jest!

In 1961, another student was tossing coins and he asked me to guess, when they were in the air, which way they would fall. This was the only time I had ever done this, and yet I got seventeen right out of the first eighteen. In 1962 I moved into a flat in Aberdeen that I shared with another student. The following day we were joined by a third student, whose parents happened to be staying in the bungalow in Ullapool where I had stayed with my family three weeks earlier.

When I was living in Harcourt Road in Aberdeen in 1963 my brother was living in Harcourt Road,

Wallington in South London.

In 1970 I went to the Welsh National Library at Aberystwyth and consulted *Elements of Cartography* by A.H. (Arthur Howard) Robinson. They also had *Marine Cartography in Britain* by another A.H. Robinson (Adrian Henry).

In 1971 I discovered quite by accident that a person who gave me a lift was the brother of someone I knew at Aberdeen University. We went on to discuss coincidences: how you often only discover them by a chance remark. Then, again by accident, I discovered that the driver worked for the Ordnance Survey in Southampton and lived a few doors away from where I lived when I worked there.

When I was working as a taxi driver in Barrow in 1996, I went to the wrong address, and one of the bosses happened to come along and told me where to go. Within an hour the same thing happened again in a different part of the town and it was the same person who helped me.

In 2001 I phoned Mr Pursey of Dicketts in Glaston-bury to ask if he wanted any panoramas and he said that he had recently been a passenger in my taxi in Kendal.

Even my name involves a coincidence. If you change the last two letters of my surname to 'us' and add the first six letters of my first name you get the most famous name from the past. If you take the last five letters of one of the titles of the most famous person from my own time you get my surname.

At one time I seriously thought that there must be

something special about me because I get more than my share of coincidences, but now I think that the explanation is that the number of non-coincidences is vastly greater than we imagine.

Barry Drinkwater, Iain McIver and myself
at the French Club play in 1963
(See page 74)

Chapter 7

College

When I started going to college I was reunited with most of the people I had admired in my past life. They were Simon Seward and Michael Dyke from Harlow College, Jackie Chandler from Daiglen, Richard Conway from Buckhurst Hill County High School and Ken Baker from the Scouts. One of the people I met at college was Pat Man, and before I knew her name I thought how similar she looked to a boy called Man whom I knew at Daiglen. This is the only time in my life that I have come across siblings, apart from identical twins, who look more alike than unrelated people.

I soon discovered that there was an organisation in the college called the Students' Union, which was exactly what I hoped that the Bus Club would become. There were meetings and speeches, clubs and committees and branches in other colleges. I found that I was treated better by the lecturers at college than I was by the teachers at school. Even my fellow students treated me better. In short, college was everything that I thought that school should be.

When I had been at college for about a month I

went to the Common Room for a meeting about how to retrieve three mascots from Enfield Technical College. There was a four-foot bear, an eagle and a two-foot concrete robot in bright colours. When we arrived in Enfield we played a sort of rugby with over forty a side but without any conversions, scrums, lineouts or rules. Every so often everyone rushed onto the ball and made a mound about ten feet wide and four feet high from which the last people usually didn't manage to stagger away before the next pile-up. I tried to arrange things so that I was on the outside and didn't get dirty. Whenever the crowd moved, I simply lifted my feet off the ground and went with it.

After the game a shout was given and we rushed the mascots into a waiting van. We didn't get the bear, but we got the other two. There were other similar raids, and on one of these I actually acquired a bowler hat that I was able to present to the Union Executive Committee when I got back. There was a tremendous feeling of exhilaration associated with these events, a feeling that was lacking from a similar event at university that had been planned in advance.

The life and soul of the college were the students' debates, and the greatest exponent of this medium was Sidney Alford. I watched him on television in 2005, and I found that he still had the same interesting way of talking that he had in 1959.

The subjects I studied were physics, chemistry, botany and zoology, but I found it very difficult absorbing facts, especially in chemistry. It is possible that there are people who have sat Advanced Level chemistry knowing as little chemistry as I did, but I do not believe that anyone has ever sat the exam knowing as little as I did *and passed*. I did this by concentrating on those questions that did not require a knowledge of chemistry. The result showed merely that I passed by a very small margin; it did not record how well I must have performed on the few questions I attempted. It occurred to me that if ever I sat for an exam that was exactly suited to me I might be capable of getting a phenomenal result. I thought that this was unlikely to happen, but it did. In an end-of-term geology exam at Aberdeen University I got the highest mark out of the 262 students who sat the exam. In fact, it was the highest mark in any subject in the university. Nevertheless I managed to fail all my exams at the end of the year.

I was an active member of the college caving club and went on two expeditions to the Yorkshire Dales, two to the Derbyshire Dales, two to the Mendips and one to South Wales. The last was to the Yorkshire Dales, when I went down Rowten Pot, which was featured in *Walks in Limestone Country*, and Swinsto Hole, which I mentioned in my introduction to that book.

On 4th October 1961 I became the editor of the Bumff Board, a notice-board on which were pinned articles submitted by the students accompanied by weekly editorials. This was my pride and joy, and the nearest thing we had to a college magazine. The following day I was appointed WUS secretary, which meant that I was a member of the Students Union Executive

Committee. The word 'WUS' (which rhymes with 'puss')
is an acronym for the World University Service. I was the
editor of the London area news-sheet, which consisted
of the back page of *WUS News*. I organised the college
WUS Week, the college carol singing and the college
entry in the London-to-Leicester Pram Race. I stood for
president of the Union but was defeated by 196 votes
to 72. I like to remember not that I lost but that 72
people wanted me to be president. Shortly before I left
I became vice-president, and in this capacity I brought
the college scrapbook up to date. I was also the secretary
of the Rag Committee, and on one occasion I chaired
a Students Union debate. The only words that were not
written down in front of me were 'carried' or 'defeated',
and I was so nervous I managed to choose the wrong
word: I would not have made a good president.

It was when I was at college that I started going out
with girls. The first was Sandra Earwaker (pronounced
Erica), whom I knew as Sandy. One Friday in 1961 I
took her home in my father's car and it was such a nice
evening we decided to go for a walk. We set off from
Aimes Green near Waltham Abbey and walked through
Galleyhill Wood to Claverhambury. The next day we got
a train to Ongar and walked to Shelley, Fyfield, Norton
Mandeville and High Ongar. Eventually I decided that
I would have to stop doing this sort of thing if I wanted
to pass my exams. When I finished my exams she was
going out with someone else.

I also went for a walk in Epping Forest with Susan

Powell, and we saw Cinerama and the film *Young at Heart* with Doris Day and Frank Sinatra. I even had the privilege of going out with Jennifer Holloman. Surely there is nothing more one can aspire to than that. We saw the film *Gigi* and we went for a ride in the car. The song that I always associate with her is 'Missouri Waltz', which has the same subtle beauty. There is a scene in the film *On the Town* in which Vera-Ellen dances with Gene Kelly while he sings about his home town: this scene captures the whole essence of Jennifer and her enthusiasm for life. This does not mean that she looked like Vera-Ellen: she looked more like Emma Cooper, who sang 'There is Love' on the television series *Highway*.

I admired Jennifer more than anyone else I have met in my life, but it was not for her that I had the deepest feelings: that distinction goes to Androulla Azas, whom I met on my second day at college, and whom I knew as Andy. All through the dreary weekends I longed for the Monday when I knew that I would see her again. Twelve years were to pass before I would experience anything like that again. I could never persuade Andy to go out with me. The nearest I got to it was to go home with her on the bus. She lived in the opposite direction from me, but that didn't stop me. The song that I most associate with Andy is '*Coma Prima*'.

There was also Teresa Ford, whom I knew as Terry. (It is remarkable how many of my girl-friends had male-sounding names.) I met her on a field course at Juniper Hall near Dorking. She lived in Bournemouth, and we walked along the Purbeck Hills from Old Harry

to Corfe Castle and along the shore from Osmington
Mills to Bowleaze Cove. I later met her at a conference
of the World University Service and discovered that
she was higher up in WUS than I was: she was on the
National Committee, and I was only on the London
Area Committee. There were others whom I didn't like
so much.

Outward Bound

In the summer of 1959 I went on an Outward Bound
course at Eskdale Green in the Lake District. I thought
that it would be a rock-climbing course, but it turned
out that that was only a small part of it. There were also
initiative tests and canoeing in the tarn and camping in
the mountains.

At the end of the course we had to undergo a series of
tests. The one I thought I would be best at was the map
test, but I spent so much time on the first question that
I didn't have time to finish it. The other one I thought I
would be good at was the intelligence test. Here I was
sure that I did well, but after the test was completed I
was told that I wouldn't get any credit for this and that
marks would be subtracted from my other results because
it was thought that people who were good at intelligence
tests had an unfair advantage over the others. In the end
I was awarded Merit, but this was not something to be
proud of because nearly everyone got merit; those who
did particularly well were awarded Honours.

Rallies

On 12th April 1959 I navigated on a rally for the first time in the family car. On 28th June I won a rally for the first time, and they said 'At last we've found something that Christopher can do.' By the end of 1963 I had won fourteen. One of the rallies we went on was organised in 1960 by the Institute of Advanced Motorists, of which my brother was a member. On this event our mileages were recorded at the start and finish, and the greater the distance we covered the more we were penalised. We tried to save three miles by taking the unmetalled road to Parvills Farm near Epping Upland, but we couldn't get through and ended up adding four miles. On the 1962 edition of the one-inch map, the unmetalled road is shown as a bridleway; it's no wonder that we couldn't get through. Despite this, we came first out of the thirty-nine starters and won a picnicking set.

One event I was particularly looking forward to was the Bloodhound Rally on 6th December 1959, because it was the first one that the college had promoted since I started going there – but when we arrived at the start there was nobody there. Then we checked the date and found that it was December 5th! The organiser had appealed for someone to organise the next rally and I volunteered. Shortly afterwards the college car club, the Octane Club, was re-inaugurated and I was appointed the Rally Secretary. In this capacity I organised the Romer Rally in April 1960, the Octane Rally in December 1960 and the Pathfinder Rally in March 1962. All these events depended on navigation using Ordnance Survey maps on the scale of an inch to a mile, and competitors had to answer questions about places on the route.

Romer Rally

This took its name from a piece of equipment that was used to plot grid references on Ordnance Survey maps. Navigation was mostly straightforward, but on one section competitors had to cross a stretch of electricity transmission line by every road that was coloured yellow on the map by the shortest route without travelling along any section of road more than once. There were seventeen starters and thirteen finishers, and the rally was won by Pat Collinson, the club president.

Octane Rally

On this event the navigation was more complicated. On one section the competitors had to find the shortest route between two points that did not enter certain parishes or pass alongside any woodland shown on the map. On another section the route had to be worked out from five map tracings, which were not aligned with the map or in the right order. On another they had to reach a point at the foot of Ivinghoe Beacon by the shortest route that did not cross any stream or enter certain grid squares. On the next section, they had to find the shortest route between two points that crossed the 500-foot contour once by each road shown on the map to be metalled.

This meant that they were constantly ascending and descending the Chiltern escarpment. The rally was won by Mr Overy, who organised the two Chingford Charter Rallies that we won. Chris Youlden and Ken Pestell (my predecessor as editor of the Bumff Board) came second, and Pat Collinson, who won the Romer Rally, came third. Altogether there were sixty-two starters.

Pathfinder Rally

The Pathfinder Rally went more smoothly than any other rally I have organised. Forty-four cars started and forty-two finished. On one section, competitors were given descriptions of four signposts with certain destinations and distances omitted. They had to work out where the signposts were situated and supply all the missing information. On another section they had to cross the River Rib by every ford shown on the map between Standon and Wadesmill. Later they were directed along roads that were not on the map and they had to give the grid reference of the place where they ended up. Many got it wrong.

On the regularity sections the navigation was easy, but an average speed of 25mph had to be maintained between controls. The position of the controls was not disclosed in advance. These sections took the competitors through many of the places I knew from my childhood in the Bishop's Stortford area.

The result was decisive: the winners had 51 penalty points, and the next scores were 134, 143 and 156. This was quite different from some of the rallies I went on in the Aberdeen area, when the navigation was so easy there were many clean sheets and George Stroud was pronounced the winner for no better reason than that his car had the smallest engine.

On 28th September 1959 I received a periodical from Fords with a photograph of myself crossing onto the island in the tarn at the Outward Bound Mountain School. On 11th November 1960 I received a copy of the *Ford Bulletin* with a remarkably similar photograph of my brother and I climbing out of a Ford car in a ford on a rally in East Anglia.

I revisited the college in 1979 and found that all the atmosphere I associated with it had gone. I expect that the same thing has happened all over the country. The wonderful films of the thirties, forties and fifties can still be seen on television, but I am afraid that the experience of being a student at the end of the 1950s will be lost forever.

Scouts

On my return from Wareham I rejoined the 17th Ilford Scout Group, and in February 1959 I went on a Scout night hike from Loughton to North Weald via Loughton Camp, Upshire and Ongar Park Wood. We were given map references, bearings and clues like 'Green stacks' for Ivychimneys, and were asked questions like 'How many taps on the drinking fountain?' This was before I went on a car rally for the first time.

In May 1960 I went on my Scout First Class hike with Ron Whitaker. We had to investigate the historical associations of certain places, starting with Ongar Castle, Paslow Hall and Torrells Hall. The farm manager at Paslow Hall had the appropriate name of MacDonald, and the farm manager at Torrells Hall had the equally appropriate name of Archer. It was in the vicinity of Torrells Hall that we set up camp. The following morning we set off in an easterly direction, but the road from Duke's Farm to Miller's Green turned out to be a river, spreading literally from bank to bank, with a road somewhere beneath it. One thing that struck me throughout the hike was that very few of the paths shown on the Ordnance Survey map actually existed. There was an excellent path from Cross Lees to Bundish Hall, but it was shown on the map as an unmetalled road. It was experiences like this that inspired me to produce (and revise) maps for people who go walking in the countryside.

In February 1960 I was appointed scribe to the Ilford District Senior Scout Executive Committee, and in July of that year I organised the Wallbury Foot Rally between teams of senior Scouts from the Ilford and Epping Forest Districts. It was like a car rally without cars and took place in the Hatfield Forest area. I wrote an article about it that was published in the *Scouter* magazine.

In September 1961 I submitted an article about a country walk to the *Essex Countryside* magazine, but it was turned down. I would never have dreamed that thirty years later I would receive a letter asking me to write articles about country walks for a national magazine and offering to pay me £120 or more per article. (I knew someone who contributed regularly to the *Essex Countryside* in about 1960, and he was paid £1 per article.)

Sudbrook

On 25th June 1962 I applied for seven jobs advertised in the *Vacation Work Bulletin,* and eight days later I started work as a relief shift tester at Sudbrook Pulp Mill in Monmouthshire. This was in England in 1962, but now it is in Wales. I used to enjoy the smell of the factory and the view down the Severn Estuary to Exmoor. I associate this view with a song that begins 'Far away, far away ...' and that was popular at about this time. In the opposite direction I could see the Severn Bridge, which was then under construction.

On 27th July I was told that my results weren't good enough, and I was sent to work in the wood-yard. At first I lived in lodgings, but from 21st August onwards, to save money, I lived in a tent at the side of a field by arrangement with the local farmer. I also got a job in a market garden to supplement my income. When I started I thought that I would be able to save £70; I ended up saving £140.

Chapter 8

University

In October 1962 I started going to Aberdeen University. I was a forestry student, but in my first year I continued to study science. In my second year I studied geography, geology and moral philosophy. I was completely unsuited to the academic side of student life: I was a very slow learner, and I found that the times allocated to exams were far too short. It was not until I started working on the Wainwright books in 2003 that I found an activity to which I was completely suited. It was about three months after I arrived in Aberdeen that I started to grow a beard.

I noticed that the rector of the university, Peter Scott, had the same name as a well-known naturalist, and when I learned that someone of that name was to address the Biology Society I wondered which of them it would be. Then it was explained to me that they were the same person, and that it was quite usual for well-known people to be elected rector. Those from the past included the comedian Jimmy Edwards and, before he became Prime Minister, Winston Churchill. In November 1963 it was time to elect a new rector. I was called upon to write the manifesto for the singer Kenneth McKellar, but I voted for the Scottish racing driver Jim Clark, and the eventual winner was John Hunt. The slogan for the McKellar campaign was 'McKellar's the Feller'. Like me, Kenneth McKellar had been a forestry student at Aberdeen and we both designed covers for the magazine *Arbor*.

When I arrived in Aberdeen I joined twenty clubs. I once received a questionnaire from one of them asking why I joined and I replied that I collected membership cards. I knew that in a few years' time I would be voting in a general election, and I thought it might help me to decide which party to vote for if I joined the Conservative, Labour, Liberal and Scottish Nationalist societies.

It so happened that a member of the Scottish Nationalist Association lived at the same address as me, and he invited me to one of their meetings. I found myself appointed social convenor, a post to which I was completely unsuited, and later business manager of the society magazine *Symbol*, a job that was much more in my line. The editor of the magazine, Irene Hughson, once confided that she was short of material, and I wrote to a number of people inviting them to contribute. I was only offered one article, which was about a group of singers who had recently become very popular, and I told the editor about it. I remember her exact words. She said, 'This magazine won't be published for months yet; by that time everyone will have forgotten about the Beatles.' Forty years later, ordinary suburban houses were being opened to the public because members of the group had once lived there.

As a member of the Scottish Nationalist Association,

I played a part in a radio broadcast for Radio Free Scotland. Because I was the only person with an English accent, I was called upon to impersonate Sir Alec Douglas-Home, reading a passage from *Private Eye*. The recording was broadcast on television after it had closed down for the night.

Shortly before I left Aberdeen I was invited to a meeting to discuss the university magazine *Alma Mater*. The other participants couldn't understand why 400 copies of *Symbol* had been sold but only 140 copies of *Alma Mater*. I made no contribution to the meeting until someone asked if I had anything to say. I said that *Alma Mater* was supposed to be a university magazine, but in practice it had become a magazine of the Arts Faculty, and I gave examples of subjects that I thought should be covered. I expected that I would hear no more about this, but after I left Aberdeen I sold some textbooks through the students' book agency and agreed to accept student magazines instead of cash. Among the magazines was a copy of *Alma Mater*, showing that they had done exactly as I suggested. In a small way I had left my mark on the university.

In my first year I was one of a team of proof-readers for the university newspaper Gaudie. Normally each of us was given a different part of the newspaper to check, but on one occasion two of us were given the same part by accident, and then we found out how many mistakes we had both missed.

Another job I had was to help backstage at the French Club play, *Dr Knock*. The most difficult task was to construct a car on the stage using various spare parts that we borrowed from local scrapyards. For a long time it seemed inconceivable that these things could be made into a car. Then, by a complete fluke, we discovered that two invalid carriages could be joined together to make a four-wheeled vehicle.

I was also the secretary of the Motor Club, the editor of the Forestry Society magazine *Arbor*, the president of the Humanist Society and the circulation manager of the university newspaper *Gaudie*, but none of these things enabled me to get onto the Union Management Committee, which was the equivalent of the Union Executive Committee at college.

Deeside Rally

As secretary of the Motor Club I was responsible for organising the Deeside Rally, which took place in the hours of darkness. At the start of the rally I was driven over the route by Ian Underwood to provide the marshals with watches and so on, but we set off much later than we should have done, and at one point we were overtaken by the leading competitor. I asked Ian to flash his lights; the car kept on going. I asked him to keep on flashing his lights; the car stopped. I promised the driver that he would not be penalised for late arrival at the next control and asked him to wait for five minutes so that we could get ahead.

Most of the navigational problems were similar to those on the rallies I had organised before, but the last section was quite different. A hypothetical aircraft was described, starting at 4500 feet at a particular place, travelling due west and losing height constantly at a rate of 600 feet per mile. Competitors had to pass through the place where the aircraft reached the ground. Had it been able to, it would have reached sea level under the A92, but it reached 300 feet where the 300-foot contour crossed another road, and that was the way the competitors should have gone. Only four of the sixteen finishers got it right. The rally was won by Charlie Miller, who was later to be my team mate on the Scottish Rally. Ian Farquhar, who was seeded number one, came second.

On the night of Saturday 20th October 1962 I navigated for James Winton on the Granite City Rally, which was the main rally of the year in the Aberdeen area; the following day I went on the Lairig Club trip to Lochnagar. I was able to do this because the rally finished at a hotel in Aboyne, and the coach to Glen Muick happened to stop at the same hotel within half an hour of our arrival. It was a beautiful day, and there was a long line of people up the mountain, almost a hundred of us.

On the night of 23rd November 1963 I navigated on the Town and County Rally, the main rally of Aberdeen University Motor Club, for Chris Burges-Lumsden who lived in Pitcaple Castle, one of the most beautiful buildings I have seen in my life. When viewed from the drive there is a fifteenth-century keep on the right and a nineteenth-century extension on the left. There is a large five-storey round tower in the right-hand corner of the keep and a similar tower in the re-entrant angle between the keep and the extension. Incredibly there is a tiny round tower squeezed into the top part of angle between this tower and the main part of the keep. There is another small round tower corbelled out at the top of the third corner of the keep. All these towers have concave conical roofs. Inside there are stags' heads and paintings all over the place, including portraits of Chris's ancestors going back many generations. We were placed first on the rally and we also won the special stage, which depended entirely on the driver. In January 1964 I met Chris when I was skiing, and he introduced me to Lord and Lady Brodie.

On 15th March 1963 I set off to hitch-hike to Istanbul, but I spent so much time in Paris and Switzerland I only got as far as Komotini in eastern Greece. After I got back I wrote an account of my travels that was published in the university Geographical Society magazine *Orb*.

From 1st July to 31st August 1963 I worked for the River Lochy Association as a river watcher. I lived in a bothy at Camisky, a country house near Fort William. My job was to look for poachers and report them, but only one was caught as a result of my efforts. While I was there, I made a note of the names of various pools on the river so that I could show these on the Ben Nevis panorama if ever I produced one. I eventually did so in 1977. I know that I was planning to produce panoramas before then because I wrote in my diary in 1959 that I had compiled a table to enable me to allow for the curvature of the Earth in the construction of panoramas.

On 28th September 1963 I went up the mountain called Glas Maol because the weather was very clear. I could see the Southern Uplands, eighty miles away. On 31st August 1964 I climbed a subsidiary summit of Ben Cruachan because I had worked out that it should be possible to see Ireland from there, but by the time I got there it wasn't clear enough. Little did I know that one day I would see Ireland at a greater distance, from Ben Nevis.

On 20th June 1964 I started working in Aberdeen as a street photographer. We used to photograph people without asking them, and if they bought the photographs we got commission. On average I only made 1s 8d an hour. On 8th July I started working for City Taxis, driving a three-door cab, and this was much more lucrative. The best time financially was around the New Year, when I made £69 in two weeks, but the time I enjoyed most was when it snowed. To me, driving without snow was like rowing a boat without a current: you can do it, but there is nothing to allow for. When the snow finally melted and I was back on dry tarmac it was like playing whist when I had got used to playing bridge.

Chapter 9

Southampton

From 17th June until 28th October 1965 I worked as a cartographic draughtsman for the Ordnance Survey at their office in London Road, Southampton. I never intended to stay there long: I wanted to gain some experience before becoming a freelance cartographer. I understood that one could always leave a job, but I didn't realise how unsatisfactory it was to do this without a reason. Since then I have tried to avoid jobs that look as though they're going on for a long time. As a result I have had a wide variety of occupations. I have spent more time driving taxis than doing any other sort of work, but I have also been a van driver, chauffeur, courier, forest worker, wood-yard labourer, farm worker, soft-drinks salesman, leaflet distributor, clerk, postman, milkman, street photographer, film extra, broadcaster, river watcher, graphic artist, proof-reader, indexer, illustrator, publisher, cartographer, surveyor and author. In 1989 I was a taxi driver, chauffeur, author, cartographer, illustrator and publisher *at the same time*.

On 5th September 1965 I saw a notice to say that the inaugural meeting of Southampton Motor Club would be held a few days later. I went along and found myself appointed the editor of the club magazine. I produced the November and December editions; then I left so that I could devote myself exclusively to saving up to buy a rally car. For most of 1966 and 1967 I worked as a taxi driver for Minicabs (Southampton) Ltd from eight o'clock in the morning until half past twelve at night, seven days a week.

The worst mistake I made at Minicabs was to take some passengers to Fawley, a village thirteen miles from Southampton, when they wanted to go to Hamble, a village seven miles from Southampton in the opposite direction. For some reason they waited until we got to Fawley before they pointed out my mistake. The boss couldn't see how I had mixed up the names when they sounded so different, but he didn't understand how my mind worked. The two names were the same length; they both had an 'a' in the first syllable and an 'le' in the second, and both villages were situated on estuaries. It was a mistake waiting to happen.

Once, when we were not very busy, I was put in charge of the office. Before long a phone rang and I said 'Hello, Minicabs'. Then another phone rang, so I put down the first phone, picked up the second one and said 'Hello, Minicabs' again. Then the third phone rang. By now I should have learned my lesson and let it ring, but I didn't have time to think. I lifted up the receiver and said 'Hello, Minicabs' a third time. Then the boss's wife came in and sorted it all out. I was never put in charge of the office again.

My longest run ever was from Southampton to the far west of Pembrokeshire. The British editor of the *Irish Post* happened to be in Southampton when he learned that an Aer Lingus plane had crashed into the Irish Sea. My longest run from Aberdeen was to Dundee; my longest run from Kendal was to Edinburgh Airport, and my longest run from Bridport was to the village of Olveston near Bristol.

Houseboat

In October 1965 I bought an old houseboat for £70 and moored it on the mud of the Itchen estuary. The first time it rained I discovered that the roof leaked all over the place. I pinned some waterproof paper to the ceiling, and this kept me dry for nearly a year. I found that the easiest way to travel across the mud was to stand on a sheet of corrugated iron on one foot and kick off with the other. Arthur New, who lived in the houseboat next to mine, made model fairgrounds. He had two sons, both of whom were called Roy. The older one was known as Big Roy and the younger one as Little Roy, but when they grew up Little Roy turned out to be taller than Big Roy.

One of the problems with a houseboat is that you have to spend a lot of time bailing water out with a dustbin. It was pointed out to me that this problem could be avoided by drilling a hole in the side of the boat and closing the hole with a bung. Then, at low tide, you pull the bung out and all the water runs away. It turned out that this was not a good idea, because one day the bung became dislodged and I woke up in the middle of the night with the boat half-full of water. My brother very kindly let me stay in his house while I dried out all my possessions.

The Grange

From March 1967 until October 1969 I rented part of the Grange, a Grade II listed mansion in the Southampton suburb of Swaythling. There was no electricity or sanitation, which meant that the rent was cheap, and, because nobody else would want to live there, I wasn't depriving anyone of a home. The house was old and rambling and ramshackle and full of junk. Among the interesting things I came across when I moved in were reindeer antlers, buffalo horns, scrapbooks from 1830 and 1915, and a collection of old maps of Southampton going back to 1611. Later I found an old fur-bound book of photographs showing the Grange in its former glory, all brightly painted and intact, when the wilderness was lawn and a swing hung from the horse chestnut tree.

The path to my front door was inclined to be muddy, and I covered parts of it with gravel that I had carried from the adjoining stream in a bucket. Outside one of my windows was a beautiful magnolia tree. Once, while I was living there, the Southampton Motor Club held an autocross and didn't have a Union Jack to start the race, so I asked my landlady whether there was one amongst all the junk in the Grange – and sure enough she found one! The song that I associate with the Grange is 'The Spinning Wheel'.

According to the Hampshire volume of *The King's England* by Arthur Mee, the Grange was once the home of Richard Cromwell, but I have not been able to find any references to this elsewhere. According to other sources, he lived six miles away at Hursley Park, where my niece Sarah-Jane started working in 1995.

In August 1968 I went to Winchester and discovered Cheyney Court, one of the most beautiful buildings I have ever seen. Other discoveries of this type I have made include Lavenham (1959), Hawkshead (1978), Berkeley Castle (1979), Chipping Camden (1984), Port Isaac (1986), Robin Hood's Bay (1994) and Dent (1999). In May 1970 I went up St Catherine's Hill near Winchester, where I had always meant to go since I saw it from the train on the way to the Isle of Wight in 1953. I also visited the gatehouse of Hyde Abbey to which the Grange was attached when it was first built and where King Alfred was buried.

Rally driving

In January 1968, I went to Stewart and Ardern in London and ordered a green Mini Cooper S for £790. When I collected it I took it to the BMC Special Tuning Department in Abingdon to be prepared for rally driving. In my student days I competed in rallies that depended mostly on the navigator. Now that I had my own car, I concentrated on rallies that were won on the special stages, and these depended on the driver.

The most important event I entered was the Scottish International Rally. I was in a team with Charlie Miller, who was leading the Scottish rally championships at the time, and Nick Britain, who was the rally editor of the magazine *Motor*. I didn't deserve to be in such distinguished company, for I failed to finish the rally because of mechanical trouble and on none of the stages was I in the top third. Ten months after that I decided that I was never going to make a rally driver, and I sold my car.

Some years later I came across a machine designed to test people's reaction times. To be a good rally driver you need to have fast reactions, but the machine told me that mine were exceptionally slow. Then I remembered playing snap when I was young. Cards from the top of a pack would be turned over one at a time and if a two was followed by another two or a jack by another jack and so on we put our hands on the pack and said 'snap'. The winner was the player who did it first. I always lost. It is not surprising that I was no good as a rally driver!

Kemp's Aerial Surveys

On 7th August 1968, I started consulting the *Southern Evening Echo* to look for a suitable job. On the very first day I read about a vacancy for a cartographical draughtsman at Kemp's Aerial Surveys, which was based at Southampton Airport, less than a mile from my home! I started work six weeks later. Among the projects

I worked on was the construction of a new London underground line called the Fleet Line, which was later to be renamed the Jubilee Line. I remember that there was a lady at Kemp's called Jean who married a Mr Jean, and so her name became Jean Jean.

Cartographic Services

On 21st February 1969 I received a note in my pay packet to say that I had been made redundant and given a week's notice. All the drawing office and field staff had been sacked except for four. Nobody had any idea why, and nobody could see how those four were going to cope with all the work. Within half an hour of receiving the letter, one of the draughtsmen announced that he had got a job with Cartographic Services at Landford Manor. The following Saturday I had a look at the manor. It was absolutely isolated, midway between Southampton and Salisbury. It was even nicer than the Grange, and bigger. The front was Georgian and the rest Elizabethan, with beautiful stone-mullioned windows. I read in the public library in Salisbury that its history went back to Saxon times.

A few days later I went there again and applied for a job. They gave me some work, which they estimated would take me about ten hours. It took me twenty hours and fifty minutes, but I was only paid for the ten hours. Three months later I went back to work for Kemps, where I was paid for the actual time the work took. This suggests to me that when I was at Kemps I was paid roughly twice what I was worth.

From the 9th to the 13th of May 1969, I travelled round the country looking for somewhere to live, preferably with a beautiful view. On my way I discovered Chester, Edinburgh and the countryside around Church Stretton. On 27th September I bought a motor caravan, the first of the eight that I was to own throughout my life, and I set off again, adding Ludlow, Shrewsbury and Tewkesbury to the list of my favourite places. When I was on the Stiperstones I found an empty cottage 1350 feet above sea level. From there I set off across the moors and came across what I thought was an identical cottage on the other side. Then I realised that it was the same one, and that I had gone round in a circle. I didn't think that it was possible to do this. When I got back, I resumed work with Kemps and continued sleeping in the motor caravan, which was parked outside the office.

On 16th May 1970, I went with my parents to High Wych church near Bishop's Stortford and found the graves of my maternal grandparents and great-grandparents, all of whom died before I was born. After that we looked for the cottage in Durrel's Wood, where my great-grandfather lived when he was the gamekeeper for Stansted Hall and where my grandmother was born, but we couldn't find it. Then an old lady invited us into Stansted Hall, where we located the cottage from a map on the wall, so we went back and photographed it. It was in a beautiful situation, nearly a mile from the nearest house. Later I learned that the cottage had

been demolished to make room for the new railway to
Stansted Airport.

Scrapbooks

At the end of 1966, after my houseboat sank, I replaced
my scrapbook with three new volumes in the form of
large guard books with green covers.

Volume 1 consists of twenty-two pages from the
original scrapbook, fifty-eight pages of maps and
drawings that I have produced, sixty pages of Bumff
Board editorials and fifty-eight pages of other things
that I have written.

Volume 2 consists of forty-four pages relating to
rallies I have organised, nine pages relating to magazines
I have produced, sixty-seven pages from my collection of
student periodicals, twelve pages of contributions to the
Bumff Board, nine pages relating to school, forty-four
pages relating to college and twenty-three pages relating
to university. There are also press cuttings in which I
am mentioned, printed maps, rally results, photographs,
membership cards, headed notepaper, licences and
library tickets.

Volume 3 consists of items that there wasn't room for
in Volumes 1 and 2, with later additions including my
collection of matchbox labels.

Chapter 10

Snowdonia

Throughout the 1970s I devoted my life to the production of a series of panoramas. The best way that I can describe this period is to quote an article I wrote for the *Geographical Magazine*.

Article published in the *Geographical Magazine* in 1981

In April 1971 I worked for the Snowdon Mountain Railway Company clearing snow from the railway line, so that the trains could get through to the summit. Throughout the winter, the Summit Hotel is boarded up with heavy iron shutters that are bolted on the inside, but there is a secret way in, known to the station master, which is used when the building is opened up in the spring.

For the next four months I lived in the hotel and worked on the soft-drinks counter. When it was wet there was little to do, but in fine weather I was kept busy handing out cans, taking money and shouting prices as fast as I could to keep up with the incessant stream of thirsty walkers.

Since the previous September I had been working on a guide to the view, and this was the easiest way I could obtain the necessary slides and sketches. The guide consisted of four drawings, each representing a quarter of the view, with the thickness of the lines varied so that the nearer hills appeared bolder and farther ones fainter, as they do in the actual view. About 500 mountains were identified, and a combination of Letraset and stencils was used for lettering. Blank spaces were filled in with paragraphs of incidental information about places that could be seen.

This was followed by *A Guide to the View from Scafell Pike,* and in the summer of 1974 I spent six weeks camping on the mountain in a lightweight tent. The ground was stony, and any stones I was unable to dig out I covered with moss. In the autumn I spent a further three months in Joss Naylor's farmhouse at Wasdale Head.

In 1976 I published a smaller version of the Snowdon panorama in colour. Woodland was coloured green, lakes and rivers blue, and paths and roads red. In 1977 I published a panorama from Ben Nevis based on James E. Shearer's drawing of 1895.

Throughout most of 1976 and 1977, I lived in a motor caravan, which I also used as a mobile drawing office, so that I could work on the drawings for one panorama while I was waiting for clear weather to take photographs for another. I found that the long periods spent in total isolation, far from the nearest building or main road, gave me a tremendous feeling of peace. In 1979, having covered the highest points in England, Scotland, Wales and the Isle of Man, I was free to select from hundreds of viewpoints the few that I found most interesting.

In order to increase output I had to make sacrifices in quality, but I found that I obtained the same satisfaction from my latest drawings, with their freehand lettering, that I got from my earlier work when the thickness of every line was calculated to within a thousandth of an inch.

The result was that five new titles appeared in 1980: Glastonbury Tor; Arthur's Seat; the Great Orme; Glyder Fawr, and the Marquess of Anglesey's Column – the same number as in the previous nine years. I also produced a new edition of *A Guide to the View from the Summit of Snowdon*, with lists of visible countries, counties, lakes and islands included for the first time, and a new edition of the *Ben Nevis Panorama*, with the Cuillin Hills and other distant parts of the view redrawn from my own slides. Some years earlier I had been fortunate enough to see everything that is visible from Ben Nevis, including Knocklayd in Ireland, 123 miles away.

I have given ten years of my life to the production of these panoramas, and now I have decided

89

not to do any more. Unfinished drawings for the Wrekin, Dunkery Beacon and other places have been filed away in my archives, along with the many interesting letters I have received. I have filled a gap in the literature of the countryside, but at the same time I am aware of how many other views there are waiting to be drawn. Visitors to the Marquess of Anglesey's Column can now buy their panoramas at the Column Keeper's cottage when they buy their tickets, but visitors to Lord Hill's Column in Shrewsbury, with its view over the Shropshire Hills, or the Observation Tower in Liverpool with its views of North Wales, have nothing to tell them what they are looking at.

My work on Arthur's Seat has introduced me to the possibility of urban panoramas. I once went up St Paul's Cathedral and decided that there were so many buildings in view it would be impossible to draw them all. I have since learned that if I drew in only a few of the more prominent and better-known buildings and left the rest blank, I actually made it easier for these to be located in the view.

Now that the hotel has been completely rebuilt I can reveal how the station master got into the building. Hidden away between the station and the hotel was a tiny door, below the level of the ground floor, which he opened with some plus-gas and two spanners. Even if someone got in there with a torch, they would never discover that in one corner, over the top of a pile of coal, was the underneath of some stairs. One of these stairs could be pushed forward leaving a hole big enough to crawl through into the main part of the building.

In May 1970 I drove my mother to Dolgellau in Snowdonia to visit one of her old school friends and her husband. They lived at the end of a long narrow lane in a beautiful granite house with five storeys including the cellar. Dolgellau reminded me of the older parts of Aberdeen and Edinburgh, where little lanes and granite cottages are arranged in a haphazard fashion. There we found a tiny terraced cottage at number 2 Love Lane, which was up for sale. It was in a perfect condition with all main services, and I bought it for £750.

Soon after I moved in I ordered some notepaper headed 'Jesty's Maps', but the only work I produced bearing that name was a plan of the ground floor of the Grange for the Royal Commission on Historic Monuments. I finished it two days before I moved to Dolgellau. The work took 112 hours and I was paid £1. As soon as I started working on the Snowdon panorama I changed the name to 'Jesty's Panoramas'.

On 14th November 1970 I attended a public meeting in Dolgellau sponsored by the Council for the Protection of Rural Wales. The speaker was Wyndford Vaughan Thomas. There was also a distinguished-looking gentleman wearing a yellow waistcoat and long yellow socks; I was told that he was Clough Williams Ellis, the creator of Portmeirion.

A week later I went for a few days to the Ffestiniog

area, where I worked as an extra in a film version of *Macbeth*. The location was cold and wet and muddy. The director, Roman Polanski, didn't do much except very occasionally run across the mud, move an actor a few feet and run back to the camera. It was the assistant director who did all the work. There I met some interesting people who talked about archery, fencing, climbing, caving, mining, steeplejacking and canoeing up the Mackenzie River. I thought how much more interesting their lives had been than mine. Afterwards I felt invigorated by the enthusiasm of the men from the film company and their determination to get everything right. Six years later I watched the film in a cinema. I couldn't see myself, but I recognised my friend George. In one scene there was a castle behind us that wasn't there when we were filming. So far as I know, the film has never been shown on television.

At about this time I sent a letter to the *Radio Times* suggesting that the manufacturers of radios, tape recorders and alarm clocks should get together and invent a machine that could record radio programmes when we were out so that we could listen to them later on. The letter was never published, and no copy of it survives. I didn't mention television programmes because I didn't think that it would ever be possible to record them.

Taxi driving

Throughout the 1970s, I spent the summers working on the panoramas and the winters driving taxis in Aberdeen. I chose Aberdeen simply because I liked it better than

Southampton. My greatest source of pleasure was the architecture of the old granite buildings, of which there is so much that only a taxi driver gets the chance to see it all. In 1977 I noted that the rate of pay was five times as high as it was in 1965, although the fares were only two and a half times as high. In 1973, and again in 1977, I revised the Geographia street plan of Aberdeen, and in 1997 I revised the Codair street plans of Barrow and Kendal, but my name did not appear on any of these publications.

In 1973 I told City Taxis that I was having difficulty in finding accommodation in Aberdeen, and they let me have the use of a large room in their office. It was furnished with two tables, a wardrobe, a wind-up gramophone, a mirror, six clocks, two penny-farthing bicycles, a tandem and a velocipede. My front door was about five feet away from where I clocked in and out. From 1976 onwards I slept in a motor caravan in the taxi yard.

If ever there was a football match in Aberdeen the streets around Pittodrie would be packed with people wearing identical coloured scarves. I can't understand why people get so enthusiastic about football, but no doubt they can't understand why I get so enthusiastic about Hatfield Forest and early Austin Sevens.

One of the drivers, Ian Bryce, presented a television programme about castles. He gave me a copy of the first edition of the local magazine *Leopard*, including his article on Pitcaple Castle. In 1978 I submitted an article to the magazine entitled 'The Little Lanes of Aberdeen', but it was never published.

I once mentioned to a lady that her accent was similar to the Aberdeen accent but not exactly the same; she said that she came from Peterhead, a town thirty miles away.

On one occasion I was one of several drivers picking up at the Station Hotel. I found my passengers and carefully checked the registration numbers of the black cabs waiting outside. Mine wasn't there! I actually said to the passengers, 'I'm very sorry, I can't take you: I can't find my car,' before I remembered that my usual car was being repaired that day and I was driving a different car!

On another occasion I was picking up at the rank at Aberdeen Airport. Ranks are usually on the left-hand side of the road, but this one was on the right-hand side. A man came up to me and asked me to take him somewhere. I saw him open the door behind me. I heard the door close, and I drove off. After about a hundred yards I had a feeling that something was wrong. I looked round and found that there was no passenger in the car! Then I noticed somebody at the taxi rank gesticulating wildly, so I reversed slowly back. What had happened was that the passenger had opened the rear door to put in his case and then walked round the back of the car to get in at the front.

Some years later I collected a passenger at the stage door of the theatre, where I knew that *My Fair Lady* was playing. From his voice and his appearance I felt that he must be playing the part of Professor Higgins. He said that he was and that he was very pleased that I was able to tell.

Hafodty

On 8th December 1970 I went up Snowdon for the first time since I moved to Dolgellau. On the summit I came upon Peter Crew, who was working on a travelogue for the Snowdon Mountain Railway. He started taking photographs of the view for a panorama to be published in the *Llanberis Area Guide*. When I told him what I was doing he took more photographs with a telephoto lens for my benefit. From 3rd April until 10th May 1971 I stayed in his house, Hafodty, in the hills above Llanberis while I was working for the Snowdon Mountain Railway. Several times people called to ask his advice on the manufacture of climbing equipment. He once said to me, 'You can do anything if you put your mind to it,' and he proved this by wiring up his house for electricity. He had ten cats and an enormous collection of travel and mountaineering books.

I knew him at his peak. His *Travelogue* and *Llanberis Area Guide* were published at about the time I was there; his *Snowdonia Mountain Maps* were published the year before, and his *Encyclopaedic Dictionary of Mountaineering* was published the year before that. In 1967 he was the climbing partner of Joe Brown on the televised ascent of the Old Man of Hoy, which was said to have been watched by fifteen million people.

At first I worked in the back of the café at the foot of the railway because the summit hotel hadn't yet opened. The best part of my day was the walk from Hafodty to Llanberis. The first section was a beautiful woodland path along the crest of a ridge. This was followed by a zigzag path with magnificent views to the left up the Pass of Llanberis and to the right over Llyn Padarn. Finally, from the bottom of the zigzags to the café, the mountains were reflected in Llyn Peris on the left.

Snowdon Summit Hotel

On 4th May I started working in the Summit Hotel, and on 10th May I started sleeping there. On 14th May the manageress arrived in style accompanied by a mountain of luggage, three dogs and a parrot. On 17th May I started working on the sweets and soft drinks counter, where I would be able to see Ireland if the weather was clear enough. I made out a list of about twenty mountains at various distances, and every hour or so I would make a note of which of these were visible. As a result, I was able to work out that the odds against seeing somewhere double about every ten miles.

There was always something going on in the summit area. On 28th April 1971 a helicopter landed and let off a great orange flare. On 12th June a geologist from the Library of Congress Museum came to collect fossils and found a rock crawling with them, although I had only been able to find small isolated specimens. On 13th June a train arrived at 6.30am bringing contestants for the Army's Fourteen Peaks Race; teams of four set off at three-minute intervals to cover the fourteen Welsh peaks over 3000 feet. On 27th June a group of VHF radio enthusiasts came up to take part in a competition.

On 9th July there was somebody on the summit who was invigilating an attempt to climb Ben Nevis, Scafell Pike and Snowdon in record time. I didn't find out until 1979 that this was Joss Naylor, in whose farmhouse I was to stay in 1974, and that he succeeded in beating the record. On 17th September a man from British Rail came up to make a documentary film. On 25th September the North Wales Mountaineering Club Dinner was held in the hotel and sixty-six people spent the night there. On 28th September some men came up to film a television commercial for Brooke Bond PG Tips. Finally, on 3rd October a large crowd assembled outside the hotel at 2.30am to celebrate the harvest moon. They went down at about 7.00am.

While I was there, thirty-eight people worked in the hotel, but there were never more than seventeen working at any one time. The highest sustained wind-speed I recorded at the summit was 57mph with a gust of 66mph.

Three weeks after I moved into the summit hotel I first saw the Lake District and Ireland in the evening. The following morning I went up to watch the dawn. I could see the Lakes and Pennines clearly. The Lake District looked like the edge of a sheet of corrugated paper. I took a photograph of the Pennines with my Instamatic camera. The photograph was too small to show any detail, but it showed the Lancashire coastline touching the summit of Glyder Fâch like a tangent to a circle, just as it does in the actual view, proving that it really was the Pennines that I photographed.

This was one of the greatest days of my life, made all the more special because it happened to coincide with one of those wonderful intervals between meeting a new girl and finding out that she didn't like me. In fact, I look on my encounter with Margot Sharp on that mountain-top as the most profound experience of my life. I remember one occasion when I had been away for two weeks. As I was passing through Llanberis I saw her in a crowd of people, and everything was out of focus except for her face. I decided to dedicate the Snowdon panorama to her, and I resolved that I would never dedicate any future publication to anyone else because that would weaken the message. Wainwright mentioned this dedication in one of his letters, and the letter was quoted in the biography of Wainwright by Hunter Davies, so Margot's name appears there as well.

After leaving the Summit Hotel I joined various schemes for meeting members of the opposite sex. The first person I met lived in Derbyshire, and we walked along Dove Dale together. I spent the following night at the Bat House Youth Hostel in Shining Cliff Wood. This consisted of a wooden hut half a mile from the nearest road. I followed the track shown on the map, but it petered out, leaving me lost in the wood in total darkness without a torch. It wasn't until long after I had given up hope that I came upon the lights of the hostel. This was the first hostel I stayed in that had three-decker bunks.

The person I liked best was in the publishing business,

which was something we had in common. I went out with her twice, which was very promising, but she decided that twice was enough. The second time I met her was in Blackpool; on my way back to Dolgellau I went to stay at the YMCA in Chester, but I found that it was full. Then somebody offered to lend me a tent. He found an area of level grass a few yards away that was completely secluded, yet with sufficient light for me to see what I was doing. He even put the tent up for me, and as I already had an airbed and sleeping bag in my rucksack I had a good night's sleep.

In 1971 I applied for membership of Mensa. I was told that my IQ was 157, which meant that I was eligible to join. It was through Mensa that I met Lyn Fitzgerald, who lived at Higher Upcott Farm near Hatherley in Devon. Her sister said that they needed someone to work on the farm, so I offered to do so, but when I had been there for two weeks I was told that my work wasn't good enough. I was told the same thing when I had Latin lessons at Daiglen in 1953, when I worked in Sudbrook Pulp Mill in 1962 and when I had typing lessons at Aberdeen Commercial College in 1964, and each time it came as a complete surprise to me.

The following paragraph may interest people who play bridge; others can skip it. The day before I left, Lyn and I played her brothers Mike and Richard at bridge. On the first hand Mike bid one heart and there were three passes. Richard laid down 18 points with support in hearts. On the second hand Lyn bid one no trump and there were three passes. As dummy, I had a look at her hand. She had 3-3-3-4 and 28 points – four aces and four kings. Later on I had 3-3-3-4 and 29 points, so, knowing the way they bid, I opened six no trumps and made it. In 2016 I read on the Internet how to calculate the odds against having four aces in one hand. From that, I worked out how to calculate the odds against having four aces and four kings in one hand. The result was over 500,000 to one.

On 25th January 1973, for the first time in my life as a taxi driver, I went out with one of my passengers. Her name was Pam Roberts. I told her that up to now all my relationships had been one-sided, and she said, 'This time it's two-sided.' It would seem that I was now experiencing something that had previously only happened to other people. She used to sing to me a song that included the words 'People say that, that you're a dreamer', which is what my teachers said about me in my school reports. In 1972 I spent much of my time looking for a person and I ended up finding one that I would have met anyway, just as in 1969 I went all over the country looking for somewhere to live and ended up buying a house that I would have come across anyway.

We decided that we would go and live in London and look for work and share a flat. It was arranged that we would work for Manpower in Fleet Street, but before we started work and before we found a flat she said that she thought it would be best if we split up. I felt that all the flavour had been drained from my life. It was like drinking water from a tap and then drinking distilled water and discovering for the first time that tap water has a taste.

Three years later I visited Pam and her husband at their home in Milton Keynes. All the houses in the area were made of something that appeared to be black corrugated iron, and they were surrounded by a sea of mud and rubble and half-bricks. I asked her how she had come to live in such a place and she said that it was because this was the only town in the country where there were vacant council houses. I looked at the mud and the rubble and the dog and the baby and I thought what a lucky escape I had had.

In the fullness of time Pam and her husband went their separate ways: the children went to live with their father, and Pam and I came to see more of each other. In 1980, we went to the South of France together in my motor caravan. I had learned from the past that it is impossible to telephone from France to Britain, but Pam was more persistent than I was. I made a note of the times she spent in telephone boxes and added them up: it came to five hours. After that time, she got through to the house she wanted, but the person she wanted was out; then she gave up.

It was not only in France that telephoning could be difficult. I once tried to make a phone call from Dolgellau to London in the 1970s. I got unobtainable forty-two times, wrong number three times (once in Newtown, twice in London), engaged three times and a recorded message telling me to check the dialling code with the operator six times. In half an hour I got through and found that the person was in all the time. It was by no means unusual for it to take as long as this.

I remember once going into a caravan site in France and looking for the office. I asked someone in my most exquisite French, '*Est-ce que le bureau est là bas?*' Back came the reply in broadest Cockney, 'Yer, that's roight, mate.'

From the South of France we went on to Brussels, where I was very impressed with the buildings in the Grand Place, and then to Amsterdam. It was here that we became separated. Pam made a note that the van was parked by the canal and went off on her own. Too late she discovered that there were canals all over the town. A day or two later I found her wandering in Dam Square and we were reunited.

From 1972 to 1976 the panoramas were distributed by Peter Crew. From 1977 onwards I did it myself. From 1979 to 1984 I was helped by Pam's sister Lynn, and I am sure that this resulted in an increase in sales.

In January 1973 I bought a Praktica camera with a 300mm telephoto lens, and three months later I took it up Snowdon on a very clear day. Among the places I photographed were twenty blocks of flats in Liverpool fifty miles away; their positions were indicated on the second edition of the panorama. This brought home to me the absurdity of trying to produce a panorama without the right sort of camera.

On 21st July 1974, after six weeks camping on Scafell Pike, I left the Lake District to sell panoramas to people walking up Snowdon. Here I experienced another spell of very clear weather, and I saw many parts of Ireland that I had never seen before, including Camlough Mountain, which would have been hidden by the curvature of the Earth if it hadn't been for refraction. My camera was being repaired at the time, and now I realised the importance of having a spare camera.

On 8th September I returned to the Lake District and enquired at the information centre in Ambleside about cottages to let. After suggesting some unsuitable places about twenty miles away from Scafell Pike, they told me of one at Bowderdale only three miles from the summit. It was exactly what I wanted, exactly where I wanted it, and my landlord turned out to be Joss Naylor, the well-known fell-runner. When I knew him, he held the record for climbing sixty-three Lakeland peaks in twenty-four hours. The following year he increased this to seventy-two. He also held the Three Peaks record (already mentioned) and the record for climbing the fourteen Welsh peaks over 3000 feet. I was there for three months. In 2006 I received a copy of the Wainwright Society magazine *Footsteps* in which the first article was about Joss and the second was about me.

On 29th September 1974 I came over Hardknott Pass at sunset. I noticed that the Isle of Man was so clear that I was sure that if I had been on Scafell Pike I would have seen Ireland, so the next day I set off for Scafell Pike in time to get there by sunset. The Isle of Man was only moderately clear on the way up, but it became much clearer as I neared the summit. Then, just as I arrived at the top, Slieve Croob appeared, followed a few minutes later by Divis. This was the only time I ever saw Ireland from the Lake District.

Once, on my way up Scafell Pike from Wasdale Head, I watched a bright twinkling light fall slowly into the sea from a great height, leaving behind a column of smoke. This was followed by another and then another. I have no idea what they were.

In December 1974 I happened to meet Sian, (pronounced 'Sharn'), who worked in the summit hotel, at Crewe, and I accompanied her on the train to Shrewsbury. This was unlikely because I rarely travel by train. Two months later I met a policeman in Dolgellau, and it turned out to be Hywyn (pronounced 'Howin'), who also worked in the summit hotel. This was less unlikely because Dolgellau, is not so far from Snowdon, but I was more surprised because I just don't think of my friends becoming policemen.

On 8th April 1975 I started renting a caravan at Pontrug near Llanberis, and throughout the summer I organised the sales of panoramas to people walking up Snowdon by the various routes. By 21st July I had people selling on all six of the paths.

On 3rd September 1977 I arrived on the Isle of Man to study the view from its highest point, Snaefell. For much of the time I was there I parked my motor caravan beside the Marine Drive near Douglas. This was one of the nicest situations I have found. Although it is conveniently situated for the town, the road is used very little after the end of the season because it doesn't lead anywhere. Whenever I felt like a break from my work, I used to walk along the drive watching the waves crashing on the rocks below and the gulls drifting on the breeze. I got a greater sense of peace from this deserted stretch of road than I did from any of the wild and lonely places I have been to while I have been travelling.

On 7th September I could see the Mountains of Mourne, Scotland and the Lake District. Two days later I could see Anglesey, with the distant peaks of the Lleyn Peninsula appearing over the top of it, but the higher parts of Snowdonia were obscured by haze. On 18th September I could see the tops of these mountains rising above the clouds, and I was able to combine the slides taken on the two occasions to produce a composite picture. When I left for Wales on 2nd November there were still one or two distant places that I hadn't seen, but I had obtained enough slides to form the basis of a panorama.

Here is some more information about the panoramas.

Snowdon

I mentioned on the panorama that twenty-nine pre-1974 counties were visible from Snowdon (counting the Isle of Man as one), and I was disappointed that I never found this fact mentioned in any book or television programme about the area. I was also disappointed that nobody has ever sent me a photograph showing Merrick from Snowdon or any other distant places that I hadn't seen, and I have never found such a photograph on the Internet.

Scafell Pike

The panorama from Scafell Pike was the same size as the large Snowdon panorama. It was a joint effort between Wainwright and myself. He drew in the mountains of the Lake District so that they appeared like the illustrations in his books, and I did everything else. Looking back, I think it is surprising that he agreed to do this, because part of the skill of producing an illustration lies in choosing the viewpoint and framing the scene, and he had no control over these things.

Some people pronounce the 'a' in 'Scafell Pike' as in 'scar'; others pronounce it as in 'score'. I prefer the second alternative because that's the one that Wainwright used. Similarly, the 'a' in 'Glastonbury Tor' is sometimes pronounced as in 'lass' and sometimes as in 'glass'. I use the first variety for no better reason than that it is the one that is heard more often.

Snaefell

Snaefell is unique as a viewpoint in the British Isles because the sea is visible in all directions, and because England, Scotland, Wales and Ireland are all visible fairly frequently. Even when it's not clear enough to see these distant places the view is still full of interest because there is so much to see on the island. Most of the peaks are seen bunched together in the south-west because Snaefell is on a range of mountains running in that direction. The most beautiful aspect of the view is the pattern made on the landscape by different kinds of vegetation, and by agriculture and forestry. The region of the Ayres, for example, is distinguishable from the intervening farmland by its dull brown colour. The farthest point visible on the Isle of Man is Mull Hill, eighteen miles away. The nearest point visible on land outside the Isle of Man is Burrow Head in Scotland, twenty-nine miles away.

The famous water wheel at Laxey is visible, as well as the runways of Jurby Aerodrome, and numerous towers, lighthouses and TV and radio masts. The lighthouses at Point of Ayre and Maughold Head are particularly striking because they and their adjoining buildings are painted white. The Tower of Refuge, the tower of Douglas Head Hotel, the Derby Round Tower on Langness, Corrin's Folly and the eleventh-century Round Tower in Peel Castle are all seen silhouetted against the sea.

Glastonbury Tor

The panorama from Glastonbury Tor was the first on which I used hand lettering, and it is the least attractive of all my panoramas. On the other hand, the view is incomparably more interesting than any of the others. I found connections between Glastonbury and some of the earliest figures from history and legend, including St Patrick, St David, St Dunstan, St Bridget, King Arthur, Merlin, Edmund Ironside, King Edgar, King Caractacus and Old King Cole. I found that the River Brue, the Glastonbury Canal, the Huntspill River, the Whitelake River and the avenue approaching the Hood Monument are all aligned with the tor, and the alignments are clearly visible in the view. Here are some of the interesting places that I was able to identify in the view:

> Dundon Hill (Iron Age Hill Fort)
> Brent Knoll (Iron Age Hill Fort)
> Fenny Castle (Norman motte and bailey)
> The Abbey Barn (built in 1330)
> The ruins of the Abbots Great Hall
>   (built in the fourteenth century)
> Wells Cathedral
> Sharpham Park Farm
>   (the birthplace of Henry Fielding)
> The Walton Windmill
> Alfred's Tower
> Cranmore Tower
> The Hood Monument
> The Burton Pynsent Column
>   (in memory of William Pitt the elder)
> The Glastonbury Thorn

At a certain time of year the tents of the Glastonbury Festival can be seen from the tor, but there is no mention of this on the panorama for the simple reason that I didn't know about it at the time. I later heard the event described as the biggest pop festival in the world.

Three times I received orders from places that I

was able to mark on the panorama. These were Wellesley Farm near Wells and the villages of Barton St David and Middlezoy.

Arthur's Seat

Among the features shown on the panorama from Arthur's Seat are:

Edinburgh Castle
Craigmillar Castle
    (once the home of Mary, Queen of Scots)
The Forth Bridge and the Forth Road Bridge
The Palace of Holyroodhouse and Holyrood Abbey
The Scott, Burns, Nelson and National Monuments
The clock tower of the North British Hotel
    (now the Balmoral Hotel)
The Royal Observatory and City Observatory
The McEwan Hall
The Royal High School building
The Hibernian Football Ground
Murrayfield Rugby Ground
Meadowbank Stadium
A dry ski slope
Six volcanic plugs
Ten church steeples and three cathedral steeples
A ruined chapel
Twenty-five tower blocks
Three power stations
The slag heap and pithead gear of a coal mine

The Great North Road
The railway from Edinburgh to London

Marquess of Anglesey's Column

The panorama from the Marquess of Anglesey's Column was the same size as the small Snowdon panorama, but the scale was over twice as great because only the part of the view facing the mainland was drawn in detail. Prominent in the view are the Menai Bridge, the Britannia Bridge, Nelson's Statue, Plas Newydd (the home of the Marquess) and the parish church of Llanfairpwllgwyngyllgogerychwyrn-drobwllllantisiliogogogoch. Three of the turrets on Caernarfon Castle can be seen in the distance.

Sales of panoramas

Small Snowdon	12,000
Large Snowdon	7000
Scafell Pike	6000
Ben Nevis	5000
Great Orme	2400
Anglesey Column	1500
Snaefell	1500
Glastonbury Tor	1500
Arthur's Seat	900
Glyder Fawr	400
Total	39,000

From October 1978 until March 1979 I worked as a

graphic artist at Chamberlain Studios in Holborn, right in the centre of London. From my window on the second floor I looked across at Staple Inn, the only surviving row of Elizabethan houses in the City. I later learned that my brother had once actually worked in Staple Inn.

Scrapbooks

At the end of 1979, when I left Dolgellau, I added a further eleven volumes to my scrapbooks. These related to the period 1967 to 1979, and became Volumes 4 to 14.

Volume 4 consists entirely of items related to panoramas including seven published articles that I had written myself, thirty published articles written by other people, ninety-two pages of correspondence, a copy of the original small Snowdon panorama, which was later redrawn because I felt that it was too crowded, a panorama of Snowdonia from Moel Famau for Mark Richards' guide to Offa's Dyke Path, a panorama from Soutra Hill near Edinburgh for the Soutra Hill Archaeoethnopharmacological Project, a list of forty-two publications in which the panoramas were featured and a list of seventy-three locations, other than outlets, where panoramas were displayed.

Volumes 5 to 12 include forty-eight pages of photographs and 135 pages of letters.

Volume 13 is a quarter-inch atlas of Great Britain with all the places I have been to marked on it. The pages of Dorset, Essex and the Lake District are covered in a network of lines, but there are relatively few in the East

Midlands and West Wales, and none at all in the Scottish islands. Everywhere I spent a night is marked by a cross.

Volume 14 is a notebook containing a list of my favourite tunes. On the first page I wrote that there is nothing more reminiscent of a time or place than a tune and that all that is needed to recall a tune is its title or first line. I felt that there was more nostalgia in this little book than in all the other volumes. The earliest song is 'Greensleeves', which was composed in 1580, and the latest 'Take That Look Off Your Face', which was composed 400 years later in 1980. In 2015 the number of titles reached a thousand. When I started to compile the list I had no idea that it would be so long.

My tent on Scafell Pike in 1974
(See page 88)

Chapter 11

Bridport

In December 1979 I sold my cottage in Dolgellau for £6500, having bought it in 1970 for £750, and I moved into my parents' house at Sunlyn, Allington Park, Bridport, Dorset. The increase in price worked out at 25% a year, or about twice the rate of inflation. My father died in May 1980, and in 1983 we were joined by my brother.

Among the things I liked about Sunlyn were its secluded position, its beautiful garden and its roof patio, which I could get to from my bedroom. Along the side of the garden was a very large beech hedge, and every September I had the job of cutting it, at first with shears and later with an electric hedge-trimmer. I was amazed at the wide variety of spiders I came across; it did not surprise me when I later read that there are more kinds of spider in Dorset and Hampshire than in other parts of the country.

If ever I found an unfamiliar insect in the garden I would look it up. This way I identified a sand wasp, a mason wasp, a digger wasp, an oil beetle, a cardinal beetle, a wasp beetle, a cockchafer, a hawthorn shield bug, a caddis fly and a scorpion fly. On two separate occasions I counted seven different kinds of butterfly on the buddleia bush within a few minutes of each other. Among the more unusual birds I saw in the garden were a lesser-spotted woodpecker, a nuthatch, a tree creeper, a spotted flycatcher, a brambling, a siskin, a whitethroat and a lesser whitethroat. In the surrounding countryside I saw a stag beetle, a glow-worm and a mayfly.

On 14th January 1981 I bought a Trendtime digital watch at Woolworth's. It was completely different from any watch I had seen before, but I couldn't make sense of the instructions. I sent the watch back to the manufacturers, but they couldn't help, so I took it back to Woolworth's, who showed me how to use it. I then rewrote the instructions so that anyone reading them would be able to use the watch. I couldn't persuade the manufacturers to make use of my instructions, but I felt that this was my vocation: I would devote my life to rewriting instruction books so that people could understand them.

To start with, I applied for a course on microprocessors at Brighton Technical College. I was told that before I could start I would have to learn about electronics, so I got a book on the subject out of the library and started to study it. I found it excruciatingly boring, and I was aware of the wonderful, fascinating Dorset countryside all around me waiting to be written about. I decided to abandon the microprocessors and devote my life to Dorset.

114

Since then I have been unable to get equipment to work on many, many occasions. I have never been able to rewrite the instructions, but somebody should do it. There are experts who are employed to help people to use computers and other equipment that they don't understand. Instead of helping each person individually, it would be far more efficient for some of those experts to publish sets of instructions that are constantly improved by discussion with the users until eventually they are so clear that anyone can understand them and every possible situation is dealt with.

My first book on Dorset was *A Guide to the Isle of Purbeck*, which was in the same style as the Wainwright books. This meant that it would have to include black-and-white sketches. I got out what I thought was a suitable photograph and tried to draw it, but the result was terrible, so I commissioned Mark Richards, who had included sketches in his own Wainwright-style books, to do the illustrations. Then one day I looked at a scene in Swanage and I felt as though I could draw it. I tried to do so and I was happy with the result, which can be seen on page 56 of the Purbeck guide.

In one of my letters to Wainwright I mentioned that I thought that the Isle of Purbeck was one of the most interesting and beautiful places in Britain. He commented that this was a surprising statement from someone who knows Lakeland and North Wales; and yet the first area of British countryside to be designated a World Heritage Site was not the Lake District or Snowdonia, but the coast of Dorset and East Devon. I have also read that more species of plants have been recorded in the ten-kilometre square that includes Wareham and Corfe Castle than in any other square in Britain.

The Purbeck guide was followed by a book of Dorset town trails. I surveyed the Bridport town trail by pacing distances and taking bearings. I laid the result over the Ordnance Survey map and it fitted perfectly, but I based all the other maps on the Ordnance Survey because the cost of the royalties was negligible compared with the time it would have taken to survey them all. The words 'Crown copyright reserved' were omitted from the map of Bridport, but I don't suppose that anybody noticed this.

My next project was *A Guide to the West Dorset Countryside*, which was similar in layout to my Purbeck guide. Later I read a West Dorset Holiday Guide and noticed that some of it had been copied word for word from my book. I took this as a compliment, but I would have liked to be credited.

According to all the books the highest point in Dorset was Pilsdon Pen, but when I was on Lewesdon Hill I noticed that the spot height on the Ordnance Survey map referred to a point considerably lower than the summit, which meant that Lewesdon Hill was the highest hill in Dorset. There were surveyors in the area at the time, so I wrote to the Ordnance Survey and they said that I was right. Mine was not the first publication to show the new altitude because it first appeared on Ordnance Survey maps while my book was at the printers.

I sent a copy of *Dorset Town Trails* to various publishers, offering to produce a book of English town trails, which I thought would reach a wider readership, but I couldn't get a publisher. The only encouragement I got was from Robert Hale, who offered to publish a series of regional books covering the whole country, depending on the sales of the first volume. I divided the country up into regions and they decided to start with East Anglia, so the fact that I was born in that area was just a coincidence. I later learned that someone else produced a book of English town trails at about the same time as I did and got it published.

The photograph I took for the cover of *East Anglian Town Trails* was the best photograph I have taken in my life. It was the right shape, with a space for the title. The Sun was in the right direction, and the photograph was crammed full of architectural features. The publishers asked for several photographs so that they could choose one. I said that I only had one; fortunately they accepted this.

While I was researching the Purbeck and West Dorset guides I gathered material for the whole of Dorset. There was no other part of the county interesting enough to merit its own volume, so I wrote about the other areas in a single volume called *Exploring Dorset by Car*. This described six circular routes, rather like the car rallies that I organised in the 1960s, and a number of walks. I featured only the best of the best of the walks because there were so many to choose from. If there was anything at all I didn't like about a walk it would be omitted.

When I produced *East Anglian Town Trails* I was happy to do my own illustrations, but some of them were not very good. I would have preferred to omit them, but they had to go in because the number of illustrations was specified in the contract. In the case of *Exploring Dorset by Car* I sent the few drawings that I was happy with and said that I was sorry I couldn't do any more before the publishers had time to ask for more.

I kept my resolution not to dedicate anything I produced to anyone other than Margot, but I gave a copy of *Exploring Dorset by Car* to Pam and wrote in it: 'To Pam Roberts, who came with me to Hartland Moor, Moreton, Ringmoor, Ashmore, Sutton Poyntz and White Nothe'.

From 1st May until 22nd May 1985 my mother, my brother and I went to stay in my sister's chalet in Switzerland. Four days after we got home my mother showed me a competition in *The Sunday Times Magazine* for a written account of up to 1500 words on a journey abroad taken in 1985, and I entered it. Nine years later I got *The Sunday Times Travel Book* out of the library. When I got it home I discovered that it consisted of the best fifty entries in the 1985 Sunday Times Travel Writing Competition. Mine was not included.

The Weald

From 12th July until 14 July 1986 I explored the Weald in a motor caravan with my nephew James. I was able to justify this to myself by saying that I was doing preliminary research for a book about the Weald, but this was never completed. We spent the first night in Staffhurst Wood, where the famous recording of a nightingale and a cello was made. As soon as it got dark a bird started singing. Whether it was a nightingale or not I don't know. The second night was spent in a sweet-chestnut coppice in Hurst Wood, where we could hear nightjars churring. Then we saw them fluttering about making strange cries and heard their wings flapping like the clapping of hands. We couldn't have wanted a more perfect spot. Later, we were driving along when a weasel crossed the road in front of us, so we stopped the van and were able to watch it only a few feet away for some time. The book I planned would have had the same structure as *Exploring Dorset by Car*. It would have included the North and South Downs but not the built-up areas beyond the downs. I would have been able to feature Rudyard Kipling, Hilaire Belloc, H.E. Bates and A.A. Milne, all of whose work I admired more than that of Thomas Hardy, who was the author most associated with Dorset.

Abacus Taxis

By February 1988 I had exhausted the money from the sale of my cottage, and I started working as a driver for Abacus Taxis in Bridport. No doubt the name was chosen to secure first place in the classified telephone directory. As I mentioned in *Exploring Dorset by Car*, this was the first time I had done this sort of work in a small town, and I couldn't believe my good fortune to be driving round the Dorset countryside and getting paid for it.

In 1989, 2000 and 2003 I took part in the television quiz *Fifteen to One*. I only got four questions right in the three programmes, but I had to audition three times, and each time only one in three or one in four of the contestants got enough questions right to appear on the programme.

My brother was an active member of the Bridport Town Twinning Association, and in 1989 he got me a job as chauffeur to the founder and chairman of the association, Peter Allsebrook. Like Peter Crew and Joss Naylor, I knew him at his peak. He was the chairman of the road haulage company TNT, which had a turnover of a million pounds a day; he was the managing director of the company that ran the ferry from Poole to Cherbourg, and while I was working for him he was appointed High Sheriff of Dorset.

At the end of 1989 Wainwright asked me to provide the maps for two of his books because of his failing eyesight. I felt like Stan Laurel in one of his films when Einstein asked him to help with his equations. This meant that I was now a freelance cartographer, which was what I set out to be in 1970. A few months later, I was asked to do a small amount of revision to page 6 of Wainwright's *Coast to Coast Walk*. Revising the Wainwright books was what I set out to do in 1980, so now both my ambitions were fulfilled, though on a smaller scale than I had envisaged.

It turned out that the 1970s were devoted to the production of panoramas and that the 1980s were devoted to books about Dorset and East Anglia. In the 1990s, as in the 1980s, I planned to devote my life to the revision of the Wainwright books. The best way that I can describe my first incursions into this territory is to quote an article that I wrote for the *Wainwright Society Newsletter* (which was later to be renamed *Footsteps*).

Article published in the *Wainwright Society Newsletter* in 2003

In 1980 I wrote to AW offering to revise his Lakeland guides and enclosing two pages of revision notes on the Patterdale approaches to the Helvellyn range. He replied that he didn't want any revision published in his lifetime, but that the *Westmorland Gazette* might be interested. In 1988 I sent a further six pages of revision notes to Andrew Nichol of the *Westmorland Gazette*. He said that he thought that the revision should take the form not of additional pages but of alterations to the original artwork. When I called on him the following year I said that he must have had offers from many people to revise the books and that I would quite understand if he gave the work to someone else, but he said that there was no question of that. I then approached AW again and, although he still didn't want the revision published in his lifetime, he said that I could start work if I liked.

This was all the encouragement I needed, as I knew that the work would take many years, and I decided to start in 1990. I was living with my mother in Dorset at the time and she suggested that we move the family home, but, so that she could be independent, she wanted to find somewhere that was near the shops, a railway station and a Mountain Goat bus stop. After looking at a number of entirely unsuitable properties, we found the house in Windermere that is now called 'Orrest End'. It appealed to me because it stood at the foot of the path along which Wainwright made his very first ascent in the Lake District. Incredibly, it also stood directly opposite the railway terminus, the Mountain Goat bus terminus and Booth's supermarket. We put in an offer, but we were unable to sell our house in Dorset, the deal fell through, and on 30th April 1990 I left for the Lakes in a motor caravan.

Four months later I had checked every feature on the maps and every word of text in the Eastern, Far Eastern and Central Fells. There was not a single path, wall, fence, building, gate or stile that had not been scrutinised. Whenever it rained I would plan the route ahead, but there was so little rain I only got as far as the end of Book Four.

Of the three books I worked on the one I enjoyed most was *The Far Eastern Fells,* for here I was on the fringes of Lakeland where there weren't so many people about. I used particularly to enjoy driving along the road to Mardale Head early in the morning in the company of rabbits and big brown owls. Among the other animals I saw were red squirrels, red deer, feral goats, a fox, a ring ouzel, a redstart, lizards, frogs, toads, golden-ringed dragonflies and an emperor moth caterpillar. Among the plants I saw were monkey flowers and starry saxifrage. In Skelghyll Wood near Ambleside I came across a fallen tree trunk. By placing one foot in front of the other and measuring my shoes, I was able to work out that it was 146 feet long.

These were the golden days. I was totally dedicated to what I was doing, and I really believed that my work would be published. I studied the books and compared them with the landscape so much that I felt that I could tell exactly what changes the author would have made to the maps and text if he were revising them himself.

By October the following year I had made all the necessary alterations to the artwork of Books One and Two. When I started on the work I thought that it would be impossible to get all the new text exactly the right length to replace the existing text without encroaching on the margins, but I found that I was able to do this. By this time the books had been taken over by Michael Joseph, who decided that they should not be revised. I was later to make alterations to *A Coast to Coast Walk* and *Pennine Way Companion* which would be published and for which I would be paid, but I would never again experience the same satisfaction that I found in the Lake District in 1990.

Throughout most of my time in Dorset life was idyllic, but towards the end everything went wrong. It started in November 1990, when I learned of the death of Pam Roberts, whom I was still seeing regularly and who was the only real girl-friend I had ever had. Then my mother started to suffer from the effects of extreme old age and my brother started to suffer from a mental condition that made him very difficult to live with. I told everyone that when my mother died I would go to live in the Lake District, and in October 1991 that is where I found myself, with no home, no money, no job and not a friend in the world. It came as a surprise to me that I would mind having no friends, for I had always enjoyed my own company, and in later years I would deliberately avoid contact with other people so that I could concentrate on what I was doing. My one consolation was the thought that, sooner or later, I would get a letter to say that my revision of the Wainwright books was going to be published, but I had been waiting for nine months for that letter, and the idea was slowly growing in my mind that if my work was going to be accepted I would have been told about it by then. The Queen once described 1992 as her *annus horribilis*. For me it was 1991.

Chapter 12

Out and About

On 28th August 1990 I received a letter from Marshall Cavendish Partworks Ltd inviting me to contribute to their new weekly magazine *Out and About*, which consisted of a series of descriptions of country walks. The descriptions were accompanied by route directions and by sections of the Ordnance Survey 2½-inch map with the route marked on them. As it is unlikely that any readers of this book will have kept copies of the magazine, I am including the articles in their entirety.

There was one place I would have liked to write about in my books but couldn't because it was outside the Dorset boundary. That was the area around Montacute and Ham Hill, so this was the obvious choice for my first article. The walk to Osmington Mills was included because, although it is in Dorset, the area is not described in any of my books. The walk to Ballard Down was included because it combines the best heathland walk in Dorset with the best ridge walk in Dorset, but this meant reusing material from my Purbeck guide.

MONTACUTE AND HAM HILL

Through hanging woodlands to an ancient encampment

The beautiful village of Montacute was the childhood home of the literary Powys brothers whose father was the vicar here. The village is centred on the Norman market-place called the Borough, which is surrounded by hamstone cottages. On the south side of the market-place there is an old plank door with iron strap hinges, and in the north-east corner there is a sixteenth- century house called the Chantry. This was the home of Robert Sherborne, the last Prior of Montacute, and his initials are incorporated into a carved panel below the upstairs window.

Adjoining the Chantry is the entrance to the vast Elizabethan mansion of Montacute House, which is open to the public from April to October. Its finest aspect is the eastern elevation, which is adorned with nine statues in shell-top niches and flanked by gazebos. This was originally the front of the house. Running along the top floor is a long gallery 180 feet long, now used to display paintings from the National Gallery.

On leaving the village the route passes the Priory Gate House, an early-sixteenth-century building of great architectural interest. Above the entrance there is an oriel window with a different carving under each of the lights, and right at the top there is a tiny coat of arms carved in the central merlon of the battlements.

The route then ascends the steep wooded slope of St Michael's Hill, the 'Mons Acutus' that gave the village its name. According to legend the Holy Cross was found on the hill in the reign of King Canute. It was taken to Waltham Abbey in Essex, which then became known as Waltham Holy Cross. The hill is surmounted by a circular stone tower built in 1760 on the site of Montacute Castle. At the top of the tower is a little room with a fireplace and four windows looking out over the countryside.

The walk continues through Hedgecock Hill Wood, where there are badger setts, to the Iron Age hill fort on Ham Hill. This is the largest hill fort in area in Britain. Within the ramparts is a fascinating area of little hillocks, the result of centuries of quarrying. The quarries yield a beautiful golden brown stone called hamstone, which was used in Exeter Cathedral, Sherborne Abbey and many famous houses. The area is now a country park, an ancient monument and a site of special scientific interest.

From the ramparts there are views to the east, north and west, and many features of the view are identified in a drawing displayed by the layby.

On the way back to Montacute the route passes through a deeply sunken lane where the Yeovil Sands is exposed. This rock may be identified by its outjutting calcareous bands.

POWERSTOCK AND EGGARDON HILL

Through hidden valleys to a famous viewpoint

The village of Powerstock lies in an area of rounded hills, deep valleys, and sunken lanes. The houses in this area resemble those of the Cotswolds because they are built of the same stone, the oolitic limestone; but the countryside here is much more beautiful than that of the Cotswolds. There are narrow strips of hazel coppice on the steepest slopes. Hart's tongue ferns and wild snowdrops grow on the banks of the lanes, and pennywort grows out of crevices in the walls.

A delight of this walk, both at the beginning and towards the end, is the constant chattering of streams in the valleys. Features to look out for are Dorset gates consisting of vertical iron bars set in a wooden framework, and hurdles made entirely of wood, with split hazel rods woven round pointed vertical stakes.

EGGARDON HILL

Rising to the east of this area, and towering over it, is Eggardon Hill, its summit encircled by the ramparts of an Iron Age hill fort. On the north side of the hill there is a narrow lane from which one can look out over an enchanting landscape of pastures, woodlands and overgrown hedges. The ramparts of the hill fort were constructed in about 50 BC, and they are much larger and more impressive than those of the older hill forts on Lambert's Castle Hill and Pilsdon Pen. From the Ordnance Survey column on a clear day one can see all the way from Dartmoor sixty miles away in the west to the Isle of Wight sixty miles away in the east. In Thomas Hardy's novel *The Trumpet-Major* Eggardon Hill is called 'Haggerdon'. It is now owned by the National Trust.

POWERSTOCK CASTLE

From Eggardon Hill the route descends to a later earthwork, the Norman motte and bailey known officially as Powerstock Castle and unofficially as 'Humpy Castle'. There is a tradition that King Athelstan had a palace on this site, and King John had a hunting lodge here. The motte was built on the oolitic limestone, and consequently it has been considerably disturbed by quarrying, but this is a small price to pay for the beautiful stone cottages that are found throughout this area.

BALLARD DOWN

Through the Dorset heath and along
a hogsback ridge

The so-called Isle of Purbeck (which is not an island) is
bounded by the English Channel to the south and east,
by Poole Harbour and the River Frome to the north, and
by the little stream called Luckford Lake to the west.
As a result of the underlying geology, the area may be
divided into four natural regions, each running from west
to east. In the north is a relatively level area of heathland
on the Bagshot beds. To the south of this is a long narrow
ridge of chalk called the Purbeck Hills. Then there is a
valley of Wealden clay, and finally there is an upland area
of Purbeck and Portland beds which presents a rocky
coastline to the south. The walk described here combines
the sombre beauty of the heath with the more dramatic
beauty of the Purbeck Hills.

The Purbeck Hills are crossed by only two streams,
the Wicken and the Byle, and between the two is a
steep-sided hill crowned by the gaunt ruins of Corfe
Castle. The keep was built early in the twelfth century,
and various additions were made in the thirteenth and

fourteenth centuries. The castle has been ruined since 1646, but two of the towers were inhabited in the eighteenth century. The village of Corfe Castle, which lies to the south of the ruins, is one of exceptional beauty. Not only the walls, but even the roofs of its cottages are made of Purbeck stone. Other Purbeck-stone villages in the area are Worth Matravers, Langton Matravers, Church Knowle and Kingston.

To the north of the Isle of Purbeck is Poole Harbour, a large natural inlet linked to the sea by an entrance only a quarter of a mile wide. The shore is fringed with sea club rush and sea lavender (which has little blue flowers). Sea purslane grows along the margins of creeks, and farther out the mud flats are covered in rice grass. The birds most commonly seen here are oystercatchers, shelducks, black-headed gulls and curlews.

The only island of any size in the harbour is Brownsea Island, where red squirrels are found and where the first Boy Scout camp was held in 1907. There is also Round Island, where Sir Thomas Beecham wrote the biography of Delius; Long Island, which was used as a hideout by Harry Paye the pirate; Green Island, which was formerly used as a pottery, and Furzey Island, which is now used for the extraction of oil by B.P.

In the Middle Ages the Isle of Purbeck was an important source of marble, which was transported from Corfe Castle to Poole Harbour, and thence by sea to cathedrals all over the country. The Purbeck Marblers' Road can still be traced, and is the subject of a poem by Bevan Whitney.

In 1982 some of the most beautiful scenery in Dorset was bequeathed to the National Trust by Ralph Bankes of Kingston Lacy. This was the greatest gift ever made to the trust, and it included Studland Heath, Ballard Down, Corfe Castle and village, part of the south coast of Purbeck, Hartland Moor, Kingston Lacy house, Badbury Rings and Holt Heath.

THE DORSET HEATH

The Dorset Heath plays a prominent part in Thomas Hardy's novel *The Return of the Native*, where it is called 'Egdon Heath'. In Hardy's day it extended almost continuously from his birthplace near Dorchester to the sea at Studland, but now much of it has been reclaimed for agriculture or forestry, or used for the extraction of gravel. More recently oil has been obtained from the heath, and the Wytch Farm Oilfield is the most productive in the country. Another product of the heath is ball clay, which is sent to the potteries at Poole and Stoke-on-Trent. Disused clay pits make attractive small lakes, the best known of which is the Blue Pool.

Among the more interesting plants of the heath are bog myrtle, also called sweet gale on account of its delightful scent, cotton grass, heath spotted orchid, marsh gentian and royal fern. Sphagnum moss grows in the bogs, along with jointed rushes and sundew. The less acid bogs are dominated by black bog-rushes, which may be identified by the black tufts about an inch from the top of their stems.

All six British reptiles occur on the heath – adder, grass snake, smooth snake, slow-worm, common lizard and sand lizard, but the smooth snake and sand lizard are rare. Roe deer are often encountered, especially early in the morning or in the evening; and sika deer are found in the forestry plantations. The bird for which the heath is most famous is the Dartford warbler, but this is not often seen. A much commoner bird is the stonechat, which is frequently seen perching on gorse bushes. As dusk falls on the heath in summer the churring of a nightjar can usually be heard, the pitch of its note changing slightly whenever the bird turns its head.

Characteristic butterflies of the heath are the grayling, a large butterfly with a habit of aligning itself with the Sun so that it casts no shadow, and the silver-studded blue, which is difficult to distinguish from the common blue. The silver-studded blue is most often seen in July, and the grayling in late July and August. Dragonflies can be seen wherever there is water, including the blue emperor dragonfly. Entomologists come to look for the heath grasshopper, the large marsh grasshopper and the bog bush-cricket, but these are likely to be missed by the ordinary visitor. Much commoner is the tiger beetle, which is green with yellow spots.

Studland is noted for its church, which retains many Norman features including two rib-vaulted ceilings. To the south of the church is a stone cross bearing the inscription 'Spaceship Earth' and the date 1976. The most remarkable building in the village is the Manor

House, which is embellished with an enormous number of tiny stone-roofed gables.

Extending to the north from the village to the mouth of Poole Harbour is a magnificent sandy beach backed by sand dunes. Behind the dunes is the lake called the Little Sea, which was joined to the sea until 1850. On the shore of the lake are hides where people can watch the water birds without disturbing them.

On leaving Studland the route passes through an attractive birch wood and crosses a little stream where hard ferns grow at the water's edge. These ferns are easily recognisable because they have two different types of frond; only the upright fronds have gaps between the pinnae.

When it leaves the wood the path crosses the finest area of heathland in Dorset. Pale grey sand is exposed, and this becomes dark grey farther on. The dominant plant is heather, broken up by patches of gorse and bracken, with cross-leaved heath in the wetter areas. Purple moor grass also grows here, and in late summer the yellow flower-spikes of bog asphodel rise from the marshy area to the left of the path. The best time to see the heath is in the autumn, when it is a beautiful mixture of subtle colours.

The path leads to an enormous boulder called the Agglestone, 17 feet high and estimated to weigh 400 tons. Boulders this size are common in mountainous areas, but in Dorset there is nothing else like it. It is also known as the Devil's Anvil, or the Witchstone, and was even more impressive before it fell over onto its side in 1970. Here the sand is cream-coloured, and farther on the ground is littered with fragments of brown heathstone.

Before long the route leaves the heath and follows the crest of the chalk escarpment of Ballard Down, which is a Site of Special Scientific Interest noted for its butterflies. The chalk is tilted so steeply the dip slope is almost as steep as the scarp slope. This is the finest ridge walk in Dorset, with views across Swanage Bay to Peveril Point on the right and views of the heath and Poole Harbour on the left – an agreeable mixture of land and water. In clear weather the white cliffs of the Isle of Wight are visible ahead: at one time these were joined to Ballard Down. The route passes the Ulwell Barrow and the Obelisk, where an inscription (difficult to read) says that the granite was taken down from near the Mansion House in London and re-erected here in 1892. Farther along the ridge two tumuli are passed on the right. Soon there is sea on both sides and Durlston Head (with Durlston Castle in silhouette) can be seen behind Peveril Point. Just before the Ordnance Survey column is reached the route crosses an ancient bank and ditch called a cross dyke.

Where the ridge reaches the sea there is spectacular coastal scenery with glistening white cliffs and three stacks one behind the other – the Pinnacle, the Haystack and Old Harry. Cormorants are common, and the cliff top is bedecked in a multitude of wild flowers in the spring. Wild cabbages also grow on the cliff top. As Handfast Point is approached the coastline becomes divided by narrow promontories into small coves. The third promontory is pierced by an arch. Eventually this will collapse, leaving the promontory as a stack. Between Handfast Point and Old Harry is the island called No Man's Land, which was joined to the mainland as recently as 1920. There are more promontories and coves beyond Handfast Point. Here the rock is still chalk, but instead of dropping sheer into the sea the cliffs are broken up by grassy ledges and the chalk is stained brown.

Before returning to Studland the route passes through Studland Wood, where butcher's broom grows. This is a plant about two feet high with dark green sharp-pointed leaves (actually modified stems) and red berries in the winter.

OSMINGTON MILLS

To a smugglers' haunt on the Dorset coast

Lying to the north-east of Weymouth is an area of countryside where the scenery is constantly changing because of the diversity of the underlying rocks. In an hour's walk one can pass from Purbeck Stone to Kimmeridge Clay, from Kimmeridge Clay to Corallian Limestone and from Corallian Limestone to Chalk; and the rocks of the heath, the Bagshot Beds, are never far away.

The walk begins by rising up a ridge of Purbeck stone that is pressed so close against a ridge of chalk that the two almost meet at Pixon Barn. From the top of the hill the sprawling manor house of Poxwell with its interesting hexagonal gatehouse can be seen amongst tall trees on the right. The Pathfinder map shows a church with a spire at Poxwell, but this has now gone. Behind the manor the main road can be seen heading for the roundabout at Warmwell Cross, and beyond it is a view of distant forests on the heath.

The route continues to Pixon Barn, an isolated stone building with a slate roof and walled farmyard. Rabbits are common in this area, and larks are constantly singing overhead. Just past the barn there is a view on the right of the chalk escarpment leading to the Osmington White Horse. Here the unimproved pastures can be distinguished by little terraces or 'terracettes' running along the slope.

As the route descends it runs along the crest of a ridge with views on both sides. On the left you can see how the Isle of Portland is linked to the mainland by no more than a narrow strip of shingle, and on the right you can look along a valley of Kimmeridge Clay to the village of Sutton Poyntz. The white horse is also visible, but it appears to be foreshortened because of the angle.

The route follows a lane shaded by sycamores and enters the village of Osmington. Note the giant ammonite embedded in the wall of a house on the right – a common sight in this fossiliferous county.

Osmington is a village of thatched stone cottages and stone garden walls. The cottages are adorned with flowers, and valerian grows outwards from the walls. Adjoining the churchyard are the ruins of the seventeenth-century manor house where steps lead down to a very old door with long iron hinges. In this village in 1816 the artist John Constable spent his honeymoon at the age of forty. He produced two paintings of the area, one entitled 'Osmington Village' and the other 'Weymouth Bay'. As you turn into the main road you can see ahead of you a thatched roof embellished with crescent-shaped decorations called scallops.

The path from Osmington to Osmington Mills is part of the Dorset Coast Path, which takes to the hills here to avoid the built-up area around Weymouth. From the stile at the top of the hill there is a beautiful view on the left looking along a valley of Wealden beds to Holworth. The Osmington White Horse is well seen from here. This is the only white horse that has a rider, the rider being King George III, who was a regular visitor to this part of the country.

The Smugglers Inn at Osmington Mills is described on the sign board as a thirteenth-century smugglers' haunt, but the present building is not as old as this. The Ordnance Survey map shows a cliff-top path to the west from here. If you walk to the far end of the car park you can see how this path has completely disappeared as a result of encroachment by the sea, and it is easy to visualise how England became separated from France, and the Isle of Wight from the mainland, in the course of thousands of years.

The high spot of the walk undoubtedly occurs just past Osmington Mills, when the path suddenly bursts upon the cliff top, and you look out over a great expanse of sea to the hotels on the seafront at Weymouth.

Before long the path passes through a thicket that has been trimmed by the wind as neatly as if it had been cut with a hedge-trimmer. As the path emerges from the thicket the headland of White Nothe comes into view ahead, with St Aldhelm's Head to the right of it. In the novel *Moonfleet* by J. Meade Falkner John Trenchard was carried up the cliff-path to White Nothe by Elzevir Block. On the top of the nothe is a small building, and to the left of this is a much larger building. This was the home of the novelist Llewelyn Powys from 1925 until 1931.

Farther along the shore you pass the wreck of an old ship whose bare ribs are a favourite perch for cormorants, and at Bran Point you can look down on a series of ledges of Corallian limestone, which is seen to be dipping to the east.

The path passes a meadow on the left that is yellow with the flowers of bird's foot trefoil, and then it descends into a little valley. Here the route turns left into a wood and enters a world of hart's tongue fern and pendulous sedge. Hart's tongue doesn't look like a fern because its leaves are not divided up into pinnae, but you can identify it as a fern by the fruiting bodies on the back of the leaves. In the same way, pendulous sedge may be recognised as a sedge by its triangular stems.

On leaving the wood the route follows a twisting traffic-free lane through lush meadows backed by woodland. This is one of the many places where there is a discrepancy between the route of a public footpath as shown by a green pecked line on the map and the actual course of the path. In some cases this can be put down to the movement of a path (just as county boundaries often follow the long-abandoned course of a river), but in this case it can only be put down to slapdash cartography. The black pecked lines (which one has to look closely at the map to see) are much more accurate, and show every twist and turn of the lane.

Later the lane passes through another stretch of woodland, but here the vegetation is not so luxuriant as it was in the valley, and there is no pendulous sedge or hart's tongue fern.

The lane comes out onto a public road which leads up through a valley cut into the chalk. A wide variety of wild flowers grows along the roadside, but pride of place must go to the nodding thistles with their big round purple flower-heads. On the left is a quarry where the chalk may be seen dipping to the north.

Along the right-hand side of the valley there are traces of ancient cultivation terraces called strip lynchets, and both sides of the valley are covered in gorse bushes, which are frequented by stonechats.

From the top of the hill a Bronze Age burial mound called a tumulus or round barrow can be seen in a field on the left. There are 1800 of these tumuli in Dorset. Behind it, in the distance, is the monument erected in 1844 to commemorate Admiral Sir Thomas Masterman Hardy, who was flag captain to Nelson at the Battle of Trafalgar. As you descend to the next junction notice the width of the hedges on the hillside opposite: they are actually shown as strips of woodland on the map.

It is possible to return to the starting point by public footpath, but it is pleasanter to keep to the road.

SMUGGLING IN DORSET

Between about 1750 and 1840 vast quantities of smuggled brandy, tea, silk and tobacco were brought ashore on the south coast of England and distributed inland by wagon or packhorse. One of the regular landing places was Osmington Mills; and from 1790 until 1800 the Smugglers' Inn was the headquarters of the smuggler-chief Pierre la Tour, who was known in England as French Peter. He eventually married the landlord's daughter, Arabella Carless, and took her back with him to France, where they lived comfortably on his illicit fortune. Of course, it was not until much later that the inn acquired its present name.

The smugglers' route from Osmington Mills to Sherborne passed the cottage at Lower Bockhampton where Thomas Hardy was born in 1840. Smuggling had ceased by Hardy's time, but he remembered his grandfather telling him how he had hidden kegs of smuggled spirit in the cottage and cut a window in the side of the porch to look out for Revenue Officers. The cottage was ideally situated as a staging post as it was right on the edge of the heath. The route used by the smugglers, which here is called Snail Creep, can be seen to this day running north and south from the cottage.

Chapter 13

The Golden Treasury of Video

For many years I wished that there was some way that I could collect together all my favourite scenes from films and television and keep them. Then, in 1983, I read in a book called *The Complete Handbook of Video* that it was possible to do this by copying scenes from one video cassette recorder to another. As soon as I knew that I had found a publisher for my Purbeck guide and that I wouldn't have to pay for the printing I went out and purchased the necessary equipment. I decided to call my collection *The Golden Treasury of Video*, and I looked on this as my greatest achievement up to that time, because I had been helped by all the greatest actors, composers, singers, dancers, writers and cameramen. Only one factor determined the choice of scenes, and that was the amount of pleasure they gave me. Some people enjoy collecting things like stamps and matchbox labels, but comparing stamp collecting to collecting scenes from television is like comparing the exploration of one's own garden with the exploration of a country or continent.

By 2001 I had accumulated eighty-two hours of selections from 2000 programmes. Then I copied the whole collection, removing the less enjoyable scenes and eliminating discordant joins. This reduced the total length to twenty-eight hours and the number of programmes to 800. I then compiled a detailed index with over 1500 entries and categories nested within other categories. There are 49 British houses and castles of architectural interest, 237 songs, 75 singers, 44 actors, and scenes from 185 films. I finished printing the index on the day I found out that Frances Lincoln might want me to revise the Wainwright books.

In 2015 I found that while I was watching my selections I would fast-forward much of it, not because it wasn't good enough but because I had seen it enough times. So I copied the collection onto video discs and further reduced the length from twenty-eight hours to less than ten. I started with Fred Astaire singing 'The Way You Look Tonight' from the film *Swing Time*, followed by about thirty other very special scenes. After that the sequence was left unchanged because I didn't want to lose the carefully planned joins. Altogether there are about 400 scenes, with an average length of just over a minute.

When joining scenes together using videotape the second scene starts as soon as the first scene ends. When using video discs, there is a slight pause either side of the join, which makes it easier to avoid bad joins. In the latest, ten-hour version of my selections, both types of join are found.

A problem I often had was that I liked the scenery but didn't like the commentary that went with it. Usually this meant omitting the scene, but there was an aerial view of Berkeley Castle that was so good I made it worth keeping by replacing the soundtrack with music. It seems to me that the picture is the most important element of a programme and that programmes showing particularly beautiful or interesting places should be available with alternative sound tracks. There could be versions with different types of music, versions with music and no commentary and versions with just enough commentary to identify the places portrayed. I think that the best arrangement is that adopted in *The Queen's Realm* and *Bird's Eye View of Britain* where wonderful scenery is accompanied by poetry, much of it read by John Betjeman.

The best foreign travel series I have selections from is *Flight over Spain*. It was broadcast in 1989 or 1990 and has never been shown since. Why not? There must be people who have never seen it and people who remember it and would like to see it again. Does it exist in the archives of the BBC or its Spanish equivalent? Are there similar series for other countries such as Italy and Greece that have never been broadcast in Britain? There should be a society of people who can speak foreign languages and can contact people in foreign countries to find out about such series and arrange for them to be broadcast in Britain.

The best items in my collection are songs from musical films, the earliest being *Sunny Side Up*, which was made in 1929, and the latest being *Flight of the Doves* from 1971, but these are in no danger of being lost as the films are regularly shown on television and some of my chosen scenes can be watched on the Internet. More important are scenes from programmes that were made for television between 1984 and 2003, such as songs from the series *Highway*, which was presented by Harry Secombe. Very few of these programmes have been repeated on television since. It is possible that in some cases mine are the only copies in existence and that I am in possession of a unique historical record.

I also have a collection of songs from radio programmes, which I call 'The Golden Treasury of Songs', and a collection of other sequences from radio programmes, which I call 'The Golden Treasury of Radio'. Among my favourite items are those narrated by Johnny Morris and Wynford Vaughan-Thomas. The longest items are from *Uncle Tungsten* by Oliver Sax, the biography of the geologist William Smith and the autobiography of the songwriter Alan J. Lerner.

Chapter 14

Cumbria

From 19th October until 23rd November 1991 I rented the attic of a house called the Stables in Cross Lane in the old part of Kendal. To get to my room I had to go through the dining room, up an iron spiral staircase, through the sitting room and up another staircase that was so steep I had to go down backwards. It was difficult to carry things up both the staircases. The room was seventeen feet by fifteen feet, two feet high at the sides and just over six feet high under the ridge, which meant that the only place where I could stand up was in the centre. There were a lot of massive beams, some of which were very old and one of which I had to climb over to get from one part of the room to another. I could see Kendal Castle from my windows.

From 27th November 1991 until 27th February 1993, I worked for City Wide Taxis (formerly City Taxis), in Urquhart Road, Aberdeen and lived in a motor caravan in the taxi yard. While I was there I was asked by Michael Joseph to revise the maps for a book to be called *Wainwright's Tour in the Lake District*. It was about a walking tour completed by the author and some friends in 1931 and incorporated maps from his Lakeland guides. It seemed to me that the publishers were scraping the bottom of the barrel to produce yet another book about Wainwright when there were two completed volumes of the revised Lakeland guides that were urgently needed and all ready to be printed. Not only that, but they wanted me to start work in October, a most unsuitable time of the year. Of course, I did it; I would rather do this than nothing at all, but I couldn't see the sense of it. I was in the Lake District from 21st October until 13th December 1992, and in all that time I only had two fine days.

Barrow

In February 1993 I left Aberdeen to live in a freehold flat at 73 Ferry Road, Barrow-in-Furness, which I bought for £7500. Ferry Road also happens to be the name of the first road featured in my first book. The flat was chosen for no other reason than that it was the cheapest property I had seen advertised anywhere. Nevertheless, I liked it better than many more expensive properties that I had looked at. The flat was on the first floor, with its own front stairs, back stairs, back yard and outbuildings. When I moved in, the flat was completely surrounded by buildings of the shipyard, but some of them were demolished while I was there, revealing a view of the Walney Channel. Sometimes I would watch enormous pieces of shipbuilding equipment being moved along the road outside. This was the first time in my life that I had my own bath and hot-water system.

In the 1990s I produced maps and indexes and read the proofs for books by Mike Harding, Bob Allen and David Maughan. I also wrote a book of predictions that I called *The Third Millennium*, but I didn't try to get it published because it only came to 6700 words, which is too short for a book, and I was not prepared to pad it out with less interesting material as many authors do. I sent a copy to Arthur C. Clarke, and I was surprised to receive a detailed reply discussing many of the points I had raised.

Africa

In March 1995 I drove to Morocco and back in a motor caravan and made a twenty-minute video of my journey, which I called *Faraway Places*. I chose Morocco because it was the nearest place that I thought would be completely different from Britain, and because I went to Greece in 1963 and wanted to set off in a different direction. I planned the video so that most of the commentary relates to the picture that is on the screen at the time, unlike many television programmes which are like radio programmes with pictures added later. I only showed myself once, so that people can see what I look like. Most television travel programmes show far too much of the narrator.

Viewfinder Panoramas

The last time I visited the outlets to distribute panoramas was in 1995. At the very last shop I went to I was shown a panorama from Snowdon that had been produced the previous year by Jonathan de Ferranti using a computer. Ever since I started work on my panorama in 1970 I had wondered if I should ever come across someone else who was doing the same thing, and this was the first time that this had happened. I couldn't buy one because there was only one copy in the shop, but I was able to send off for a catalogue. Having taken ten years to produce ten panoramas, I was astonished to discover that Jonathan could produce one from the Ordnance Survey database in thirty minutes, and that he had already produced panoramas from 127 places in the British Isles.

I had used a pocket calculator to work out the outlines of very distant mountains that I had been unable to see, and I thought that it might be possible to do this more quickly using a computer, but I assumed that one would still have to plot the outline on a piece of graph paper and copy it onto the panorama. It never occurred to me that a computer could actually draw the outlines.

For many reasons I was sure that Jonathan had not consulted my publications when producing his own, and it was therefore a fascinating exercise to place the two panoramas side by side and compare them. The first thing that struck me was that in those places where I had gone to great lengths to get everything right the two panoramas were exactly the same. This gave me confidence that wherever there was a discrepancy between the two panoramas it was mine that was inaccurate. It was like taking an examination and later seeing the answers – but on this occasion I had to wait for more than twenty years for the answers.

The panoramas are encased in transparent plastic, so that they are waterproof, washable and extremely tough. Different colours are used to indicate distances, and the sky is pale blue. The drawings on the back are printed upside down, which is sensible because it is easier to turn the panoramas over vertically than horizontally. Bearings are shown in degrees, and I couldn't find a single instance where a mountain was wrongly identified or a distance miscalculated by more than a mile.

From June 1995 until May 1996, I worked for JC Taxis in Barrow. On 6th February 1966 there was ten inches of snow on the ground outside my flat and twenty-four inches in the countryside. Over the next two days my average hourly takings were double what they usually were and my tips were four times as great.

In December 1996 I started working as a taxi driver in Kendal, which meant that I had to drive from Barrow to Kendal and back every day. To avoid this, in December 1998 I moved into a rented flat at number 5 Chapel Close, Kendal. It was on the top floor of a former mansion, and it had a wonderful view: I had finally found the home with a view that I was looking for in 1969. To get from the town centre to my flat I had to climb over a hundred steps.

At first I tried letting my flat in Barrow, but I found that this was so much trouble that in 2000 I decided to sell it. This took ten months, and all I got was £5000, two thirds of what I paid for it. In 2007, I was paying £98 a week for a cottage in Kendal that was sold for £117,000. This represented a return of only 4.4% per year. The £42.50 a week rent I received for my flat in Barrow represented 44% per year of the £5000 I sold it for.

While I was living in Barrow and working in Kendal the best part of my day was the journey to and from work via Underbarrow, and the best of this was captured by a video camera so that I could enjoy it in later life. After I moved to Kendal, I filmed the view of the countryside from my flat in Chapel Close. Then I made another video of the buildings of the town from the same place while the Town Hall bells were chiming 'The British Grenadiers'. I chose to switch the camera on as the bells started, but the fact that they finished just as the video finished was sheer good luck. Because I was looking down on the town at an angle the shop fronts and the people and traffic were all hidden from view.

Castle Taxis

From July 1997 until June 2003 I worked for Castle Taxis in Kendal, a period of nearly six years. This was over twice as long as my second-longest job and over six times as long as my second-longest full-time job. While I was driving around I saw a pair of multi-coloured mock suns, one each side of the real sun. I also saw people walking on stilts, a unicycle, a tandem for three people, a steam-driven lorry, the actual car that was used in the film *Chitty Chitty Bang Bang* and a dark green D-type Jaguar that not only looked beautiful but sounded beautiful as well. One day in 1999 I received a £5 coin for the first time and immediately put it back into circulation because I expected to receive hundreds of them, but I have never seen one since.

Sometimes, if I started early in the morning, I would be the only person working; I would drive the car and answer the telephone using a mobile phone. When I did this one of two things usually happened: either I would tell the customer that we were fully booked, put the phone down and then work out that the job they wanted me to do fitted in nicely with existing jobs, or I would accept a job, put the phone down and then realise that the job didn't fit the schedule at all, so that I would be running late from then onwards. Occasionally I would have two cars to control, and this was too complicated for me, yet Jimmy McIntosh in Aberdeen could control eighty cars at once and he never made a mistake.

When I was a taxi driver I was always pleased if someone asked me the way to somewhere; the other person might be more knowledgeable than me in most subjects, but in this particular situation I was the expert.

In the income tax year 1998-9 I noted that my average income from taxi driving was £113 a week, which was £79 less than the minimum wage for the hours I worked.

In August 1999 I was asked to leave my flat in Chapel Close, but I found an even better one in a house that

I had long admired at 24B Beast Banks, Kendal. It stood at the start of the first walk in *The Outlying Fells of Lakeland* (except for a short stretch that was shared by the outward and return journeys). The windows looked out across a perfect village green; the sitting room had a low ceiling and beautiful wallpaper, and there was a turret that was used as a kitchen. Before I went to look at the flat I had to take some luggage in the taxi to a house in Bowness. It took me an hour and a half to find it, and I arrived at Beast Banks with not a minute to spare. It was as well that I eventually found the house in Bowness because someone else had arranged to look at the flat a quarter of an hour after me!

I later learned that the post office four doors along from my house was the inspiration for the Postman Pat series of books. It has since been closed down.

In 2001 I bought a leaflet about a geological walk in Kendal that pointed out fossils all over the town that I hadn't noticed before. I used to love exploring the alleyways of Kendal, and without making any effort to do so I found myself arranging them to make a circular walk that started and finished at the town hall. I printed out a description of the walk and gave a copy to anyone who was interested. In 2002 I donated the originals of the Wainwright correspondence to the Kendal Museum.

I conclude this chapter with some letters I wrote at about this time.

Letter published in *The New Scientist*, 2nd June 1994:

Universal happiness

In the edition of May 28th you published a letter from Alison Brooks saying that there are people who believe that the general level of happiness can be raised by the improvement of social conditions. Don't such people realise that improvements of this sort can only make people happier until the novelty wears off and the new conditions become the norm?

The only way that the average level of happiness can be raised in the long term is by discovering the physical or chemical processes that underlie changes of mood and learning to control them. If ever this happens it will be, quite simply, the greatest discovery in the history of the world.

Letter published in *Punch*, 11th September 1996:

In view of the confusion that sometimes arises over the periods of English architecture, I thought you might like to publish the following explanation:

English architecture may be divided into Roman, Saxon, Norman, Early English, Decorated, Perpendicular, Tudor, Georgian and Victorian. Roman architecture is that of Rome, which is in Italy, and therefore not found in England. Saxon architecture is that of Saxony, which is in Germany, and therefore not found in England. Norman architecture is that of Normandy, which is in France, and therefore not found in England. Early English architecture is everything that was built in England before 8.00 in the morning. Decorated is self-explanatory and refers to everything built in England except for twentieth-century council houses, which are undecorated. Perpendicular is likewise self-explanatory and refers to everything built in England, the one building that is not perpendicular being the Leaning Tower of Pisa, which is in Italy. Tudor architecture is that built by Henry VII, Henry VIII and Elizabeth I, but as none of these was a builder, it is not found in England. Georgian and Victorian architecture are not found in England for the same reason.

I hope that this clears everything up.

This is the version that was submitted; the published version was slightly different and, in my opinion, not so good. In 1996 I wrote to Jim Watson, the author of a book of Lakeland panoramas, and received a reply saying that the day he got my letter he read my article in *Punch*. If he hadn't noticed it I would probably never have known that the article had been published.

To the *Guinness Book of Records*, 21st July 1996:

From 1970 until 1979 I devoted my life to the production of a series of guides to the views from mountaintops in Britain. In the 1980 edition of the Snowdon panorama I wrote that I had come to the conclusion that the greatest distance visible on land anywhere in Britain is that from Snowdon to the Merrick in southern Scotland. The distance is 231.87 km, or 144.08 miles.

For many years mine were the only publications of this type available. Then, in 1994, Jonathan de Ferranti started producing panoramas in greater numbers using a computer. He also worked out that the greatest distance visible in Britain is that from Snowdon to the Merrick, although at the time he had not seen any of my panoramas.

With two people arriving independently at the same conclusion, it seems to me that this record should now be regarded as a fact, and I wondered if you might consider it worth mentioning in the *Guinness Book of Records*.

To the *Guinness Book of Records*, 7th October 1997:

On reading the 1998 edition of the *Guinness Book of Records* I was very pleased to see that you were able to mention on page 214 that the greatest distance visible in Britain is that from Snowdon to the Merrick. On the other hand, I was very disappointed to see that the distance is given as 144.08 km or 89.5 miles. In my letter of 21st July 1996 I made it clear that the distance is 231.87 km or 144.08 miles. A quick glance at any small-scale map would be sufficient to show that 89 miles is too short. Norris McWhirter would never have let a mistake like that get through. Jonathan de Ferranti shows Snowdon on his Merrick panorama, but he does not show the Merrick on his Snowdon panorama because he feels that it is too close to Lamachan Hill to be distinguishable. I therefore suggest that in the next edition the paragraph should be rephrased: 'The longest line of sight in the British Isles is 231.87 km (144 miles). In exceptionally clear weather it is possible to see Snowdon, Gwynedd, Wales from the summit of the Merrick, Dumfries and Galloway, Scotland.'

The record was never mentioned again in the book.

To Answers Please, the *John Dunn Show*, Radio 2, 4th September 1996 (not broadcast):

The recent repeat of a radio programme made by Percy Edwards in the 1970s means that there must exist in the BBC a recording of that programme. Do recordings exist of all radio programmes, or only some of them? Are there any records of which programmes have been kept and which have been lost? Are these records accessible to members of the public?

In the past ten or fifteen years nearly all the films that I remember from my youth have been shown on television, even those which the reviewers regard as being not worth seeing. When are we going to hear all the old radio programmes again?

In the next three letters the questions were provided by other readers of *The New Scientist* magazine, and I suggested appropriate answers, but none of them was published.

To The Last Word, *The New Scientist*, 6th August 1994:

Q: Can anyone explain in simple and common-sense terms why there is simultaneously a high tide on both sides of the Earth?

A: Many people are puzzled by this but the explanation is really quite simple. On the side of the Earth closest to the Moon the water is attracted to the Moon slightly more than the Earth as a whole because it is nearer. Therefore the sea swells up on that side. On the side of the Earth farthest from the Moon the water is attracted to the Moon slightly less than the Earth as a whole because it is farther away. Therefore the sea on that side also swells up.

To The Last Word, *The New Scientist*, 20th February 1995:

Q: Why do people say 'um'or 'er'when hesitating in their speech?

A: 'Um' and 'er' are the two most undervalued words in the English language. They mean 'Don't say anything, I'm thinking what to say next.' The two seconds' thinking time that results is nothing like long enough, but it is better than nothing.

To The Last Word, *The New Scientist*, 4th November 1995:

Q: Is it true that the living outnumber the dead? A: The number of people living is now about five or six thousand million. This number can never catch up with the number of dead people, which is now around a hundred thousand million. If the population levels off at ten thousand million and the Earth remains inhabitable for a thousand million years, as is thought likely, the people of the past and present will be outnumbered by those who are yet to be born by a factor of about a million. The story of the human race is only just beginning.

Letters to the Editor, *The New Scientist*, 20th January 1998:

(This letter was not published, but there was a letter from someone else making the same point.)

> In the article 'That's amazing, isn't it?' the authors claim that the number of games of bridge played worldwide is so huge that every few weeks a hand may be expected to occur in which each player is dealt a complete suit. This is quite impossible, because the odds against it happening are of the order of 10^{27} to one against, whereas the number of hands dealt in the course of a year is no more than 10^{10} or 10^{11}. It is quite possible, however, that once every few weeks someone switches a carefully sorted pack of cards with one that has just been shuffled while the attention of the players is diverted.

I might have added that anyone doing this should ensure that when a hand is picked up the cards are not in numerical order. If the ace is followed by the king and then the queen and so on nobody will believe that it was accidental.

Chapter 15

So Much to Say

In 1999 I copied the best of my writings onto a computer disc, which I called 'So Much to Say', and which I gave to people I knew who had computers. This included published and unpublished writings, personal information, correspondence, selected passages from books, diaries and childhood photographs. I think that the best part consisted of ideas that come to me from time to time and that I feel are so profound that they should be written down for other people to read. Here are some examples.

It's a miracle that language and civilisation have evolved; it's a bigger miracle that life has evolved from non-living matter, and it's a bigger miracle still that the Universe has come into existence from nothing. The population of the world is greater than it has ever been; the average lifespan is longer than it has ever been; if we ignore minor fluctuations the average standard of living is higher than it has ever been – and yet people still find things to complain about. It seems to me that what is wrong is not the things that people complain about, but the fact that they do so.

Think how lucky we are that there happen to be light and sound waves in the air and that we have evolved to make use of them. If it hadn't been for hearing, we would not only have been denied the pleasure of listening to music, we would have been unable to engage in conversation and share our ideas; there would have been no civilisation.

There are more insects in the world than people, and it is much more likely that you would have been born an insect than a person. If you had been born in the first 99.9% of the Earth's existence, it would not only have been unlikely that you would be a human being, it would have been impossible.

Look back on your past life. Think of all the enjoyable experiences you have had and all the worthwhile things you've done. Multiply that by a hundred thousand million, and you have the story of the human race.

When I'm in a good mood, I feel that I live in a wonderful world and I know that I do; when I'm in a bad mood I don't feel that I live in a wonderful world but I still know that I do.

I have come to the conclusion that the range of pleasant and unpleasant experiences that make up life is unaffected in the long term by changes in circumstances. If you dislike something and the thing you dislike disappears from the face of the Earth, sooner or later you will find something else to dislike in exactly the same way and to exactly the same extent.

If you dislike something that has been caused by

other people it means that somebody must like it, and if you believe that other people are just as important as you are it follows that putting right the thing you think is wrong will make things no better and no worse than they are already.

It is possible that human civilisation will survive for a thousand million years. If it does not last that long then it must go into a period of decline, in which case the people of the future will look back on the present time as a golden age.

There is no evidence that other people experience colours and tastes the same way that I do. In fact there is some evidence that they don't. Some people choose to wear clothes that I find unattractive; some people choose to eat food that I don't like, but they must like the taste. This doesn't necessarily mean that it tastes differently to them, but it suggests that this is likely. There is no way of finding out.

I can understand how muscles make the arms move. I can imagine being able to understand how nerve impulses make the muscles contract. I can't even imagine being able to understand how I control the nerve impulses.

If there were no people in the Universe, there would be no art or literature, but there would still be biology. If there were no life in the Universe, there would be no biology, but there would still be physics and chemistry. If there were no Universe, there would be no physics or chemistry, but there would still be mathematics. It might be said that there could be no mathematics if there were no numbers and that there could be no numbers if there were no material objects to count, but I believe that mathematics exists independently of the Universe because I can imagine a universe in which the mass of a proton is not 1836 times that of an electron, but I cannot imagine a universe in which 2 x 3 does not equal 6.

Extra-terrestrial life is an interesting question because it is possible that it exists and it is also possible that it doesn't exist. Ghosts pose an even more interesting question because it is impossible that they exist and it is equally impossible that everyone who claims to have seen one is pretending.

Animals are alive, which means that they are aware of their existence. We are told that plants also are alive. Does that mean that they also are aware of their existence? If not, where do we draw the line? I am sure that dogs and cats are aware of their existence, but what about tortoises? What about goldfish or earwigs or snails? What about microscopic animals that are virtually indistinguishable from plants? A doctor was once asked if it was possible that plants feel pain, and he said that it wasn't possible because plants have no nervous system – but surely you don't need a nervous system to feel thirsty. If an animal feels thirsty when its body needs water, then why shouldn't a plant do the same? And if it feels thirsty it must be aware that it feels thirsty and therefore aware that it exists. [I thought that I was the only person to think on these lines until I read something similar in a book called *What Does It All Mean?*]

Money is a peculiar thing. People only want it because they can buy things with it. But the people they buy things from only want it so that they can buy things from other people, and so on. So how does it all start?

The metric system is sometimes said to be completely rational and logical but that is not entirely the case. One hears about hectares but not decares, decibels but not centibels, and milliseconds but not kiloseconds.

If you float a beach ball on the sea when there is an offshore breeze, the ball will go up and down with the waves and move away from the shore at the same time. So why do some people have difficulty in visualising a photon as a wave and a particle at the same time?

It should be possible to look at human civilization objectively, not just to know how remarkable it is but to feel it. Imagine someone who lived a hundred thousand years ago and who was trying to build a primitive shelter and wondered if there would ever come a time when people lived in waterproof houses with transparent windows and lights you can switch on and off. You don't have to wonder if it all came about; you know that it did. Now imagine that you were born in the twentieth century but had spent all your life in a box six feet square with plain walls and that a few seconds ago you walked out of that box for the first time. Imagine discovering that there are other people like yourself, and that there are rows of houses and books and films and television programmes containing limitless information. We all know what there is to discover, but we are so familiar with it that most of us take it all for granted.

I believe that my sense of wonder is greater than that of the average person, but I know that it is nothing like as great as it should be. Every moment of every day I should be thinking things like 'Isn't it incredible: that electric light really works!' or 'Water really does come out of that tap!' or 'That amazing adventure that began in 1942 really is still going on!'

I have always believed (1) that the mind can be explained by the arrangement of atoms in the brain, and (2) that a computer cannot have a mind. Then one day I realised that these two opinions are inconsistent. The second must be right, therefore the first must be wrong.

Galaxies, quarks and so on are important to the human race because they provide an endless supply of interesting things for people to find out about.

We are led to believe that there is nothing special about the world: it's just an ordinary planet going round a typical star in a typical galaxy. In the same way, it might be said that there is nothing special about the present time: the Earth has been going round the Sun for thousands of millions years, and it will continue to do so for thousands of millions of years to come. On the other hand, it could be said that there has been as much progress in the last hundred years as there was in the previous thousand years, and that there has been as much progress in the last thousand years as there was in the previous ten thousand years, and so on. Surely this can't go on forever, so we must be living in a special time.

The Earth is a planet 8000 miles across in a universe that extends for millions of millions of miles in all directions. It therefore could be said that nothing that happens on that planet can be of any possible significance

168

– but it is of the greatest significance to the people who live there. In the same way, it may be said that in a world inhabited by millions of people nothing that happens to one individual can be of any significance, but it is of the greatest significance to that person. If you believe that the human race is important, you should also believe that your own life is important even if your rôle in the world is a very small one. If you believed that you were the only person in the world you would not consider your life to be so insignificant. And if you then discovered that there were millions of other people in the world, your life would be greatly enriched, and if it were greatly enriched it could hardly be regarded as being less important.

Chapter 16

The Internet

In 1994 I heard that vast amounts of information could be stored on CD-ROMs, and I sent the following letter to the editor of the magazine *CD-ROM User*:

> I have often thought that there should be some way that I could find out what has happened to people I knew long ago and have lost touch with, and to tell them what has happened to me. Obviously it would be impossible to publish a book giving the life histories of millions of people, but I wonder whether something of this sort could be achieved through CD-ROM, particularly if it is likely to become more and more popular in the future.
>
> If the custom of recording one's life history on CD-ROM should ever become universal then records of everyone's lives would be left for the benefit of posterity.

The letter was never published and I heard no more about it, but in 1996 I succeeded in connecting my computer to the Internet. I looked up 'WHO's online' because I thought that this might provide me with what I was looking for, but all I could find was the occupations and places of work of twelve people. I also had a look at the classified advertisements on the Internet and found that they featured no more than three houses, a car and a camera. The only useful information I obtained was the time of a train. One thing did impress me, however: I searched for 'Jesty' in a series of 400,000 magazine articles and found a reference to someone of that name. I knew that it was very rarely that I came across my surname, and this demonstrated how extraordinarily fast the equipment could search. In December 1996 I gave up the Internet because it was too expensive and too time-consuming.

In 2005 I was asked by my publishers to make arrangements so that I could correspond with them by email, and I found that doing this enabled me to start using the Internet again. Fifteen months after I reconnected I discovered a button called 'search' that I hadn't noticed before. I used it to search for 'Chris Jesty' and to my astonishment I found three references to myself. Three months later this had gone up to ten and eventually it reached four hundred. I noticed that the house next door to mine was up for sale, and by typing in the name of the estate agent I found details of the house. This suggested that most of the houses for sale were there somewhere and that the Internet had expanded enormously in ten years.

I was only able to find references to myself because I

have an uncommon surname. If I searched for people I used to know all I could usually get was vast amounts of information about people I didn't know who happened to have the same name. My first success came when I looked up the South-West Essex Technical College and found references to Malcolm Bonner, with whom I took part in a hitch-hiking race from London to Gretna Green. Then I found out how to search for an article that includes two phrases. For example by combining 'Jack Chandler' with 'Walthamstow Stadium' I found out that he had become the managing director. I thought that this was likely because his father and uncle were running the stadium when I was at college.

Some people I was able to find because they had unusual names, such as Ole Wiebkin, who illustrated the article I submitted to the *Essex Countryside* magazine in 1961, and Harley Crossley, who was my co-driver on the Scottish Rally in 1968. When I knew him he was an accomplished amateur artist. In 2009 I learned that he had been a professional artist for thirty years, and I was able to see 187 of his paintings. Every one of them was better than the sort of paintings that change hands for millions of pounds. In 2013 I found recent photographs of both Ole and Harley on the Internet and they looked exactly as I imagined they would.

I also found Chris Burges-Lumsden, for whom I navigated on a number of rallies in 1963–5 and who lived in a fairy-tale Scottish castle. In 2012 I read that he was still living in the castle, and a couple of years later I found a recent photograph of him. I was delighted to learn that the castle was completely unchanged.

I thought that women would be particularly difficult to locate because they are inclined to change their surnames, but I found Duffy de France, whom I met at Bangor Youth Hostel in 1971, and read that she had recently met the vice-president of the United States. It was not until November 2014 that I thought of looking for Maureen Preen, who was the person I most admired when I was at the Ordnance Survey. I found a story of her life and a photograph taken not long after I met her, and I read that she, like me, has appeared on the television series *Countryfile*. I later found references to Gullan Agerbak, whom I admired when I was at university.

I also tried typing in some of my former addresses and found recent interior photographs. I was struck by how much the houses had changed over the years; I was only able to recognise my cottage in Dolgellau by the bent beam in the upstairs ceiling, and the family home in Sawbridgeworth was much more luxurious than I remembered it. I didn't expect to find the Grange because I knew that it had been demolished in the early 1970s, but there was an excellent photograph of it taken in 1909. The pleasantest surprise of all came in 2015 when I found interior photographs of my very first home, Whistlefield.

Earlier on I had read on the Internet that the current occupier of Whistlefield was a man named Christopher Goodlife. I couldn't have made up a more suitable name: the Christian name was the same as my own, and the surname was the title of my favourite television series, as well as a description of my life when I was living in the cottage.

In 2008 I looked up the South West Essex Technical College again on the Internet. I learned that it was now part of the University of East London and that former SWETC students could join their alumni network. In 2013 I read that in their archives there were copies of college magazines dating from the time that I was there, so I offered to donate a computer disc containing thirty-four Bumff Board editorials and thirteen contributions, and this was accepted.

Through the Internet, I discovered that there were a very small number of people with the same Christian name and surname as myself. One was in the Unison Football Club and another in the Thames Valley Harriers. These were merely mentioned, but there were two others, one in Britain and one in the United States, who were described in great detail. The most striking thing about both of them was they were as different from me as they could possibly be. By 2016 references to all these people had disappeared from the Internet except for the one in the United States. Then, in 2017 I discovered another living in England.

Before I knew that there were people with the same Christian name and surname as myself I would very occasionally come across people with just the same surname, and I found that I had much more in common with them. For example, Bill Jesty and I both appeared on the television series *Countryfile*, and Ron Jesty and I both drew maps of the village of Abbotsbury. His map was displayed in the village and mine appeared in my West Dorset guide.

In 2011 I looked up Bedlar's Green on the Internet and found an aerial photograph of the area showing my childhood home. To my astonishment I discovered that by pressing buttons I could expand the area of the photograph step by step until it covered the whole world. I could then choose a particular part of the world and zoom in on it. One of the places I discovered in this way was the coast of Florida, where I was amazed by the quality of the photography and by the quality of the scenery. This gave a whole new meaning to the phrase 'armchair travelling'.

The best video I found on the Internet consisted of a series of beautiful scenes accompanied by the song 'Flower of Scotland', but my most remarkable experience came on 5th August 2013, when I looked up 'British cartographers' in Wikipedia and found references to eight people. Only one of them was still living – and that one was me!

Chapter 17

Wainwright

From 2003 to 2013 I devoted my life to the revision of Wainwright's pictorial guides. The best way that I can describe this period is to quote two more articles that I wrote for the Wainwright Society magazine. I assumed that members would know that John Pulford was the treasurer of the society, that Betty Wainwright was the author's widow and that Edale was the start of the Pennine Way.

Article published in the Wainwright Society magazine *Footsteps* in 2009

When I submitted an article to this magazine in December 2002 about my unpublished work on the revision of the Lakeland guides I never dreamed in my wildest moments that six months later I would be back at work, and that this time my work would be published. I knew that both the publishers (Michael Joseph) and Betty Wainwright were opposed to the idea. I thought that I was incapable of the dedication that I knew was required, and in any case I was far too old. Then, before the article was published, the books were taken over by Frances Lincoln, who were in favour of the revision. They were able to persuade Betty that it was a good idea and me that I was capable of doing it. I started work on 2nd June 2003, which happened to be exactly fifty years from the Coronation and the announcement of the first ascent of Everest. Two days earlier I had finished listening to a serialised account of the ascent on the radio, and this was just the thing to get me into the right frame of mind for my own forthcoming adventure.

I gave up all activities apart from my work and turned down all invitations, except where publicity was involved. I would give interviews for magazines and later read that I had said things that I was quite sure I had never said. You might think that this couldn't happen on radio or television, but it can: on the television series *Mountain*, by carefully cutting out much of what I said, the producers were able to make me tell millions of people that seven plus one equals ten.

I couldn't resist the temptation to identify some of the unfamiliar wild flowers I came across, including starry saxifrage, alpine lady's mantle, bird's eye primrose, wild thyme, cowberry, butterwort, bistort and bugle. I also identified eight different kinds of caterpillar, but I never identified those I saw on 11th June 2007. I was

177

in one of the remotest parts of the Lake District, the moors above Iron Crag near Ennerdale, and there were caterpillars every few inches over an area more than a quarter of a mile across. There must have been millions of them. They were dark grey or dark brown with wide yellow stripes along their sides and five narrow yellow stripes along their backs.

I had another interesting experience on 15th January 2007. I was driving along the shore of Ullswater, well above the level of the lake, when a wave came up and completely covered the windscreen, so that for a moment I couldn't see where I was going.

On 14th January 2005 I walked through a plantation below Black Fell; there were so many trees blown down it was very difficult for me to find a way through them. There was hardly a tree left standing. I later approached the plantation from another direction and found it impossible to get through. I had never encountered anything like it before in my life.

On another occasion I went up Rosthwaite Fell from Stonethwaite. In the valley the fields were so white with frost it looked like snow. Everything was covered in spikes of ice a quarter of an inch long. In the afternoon I watched dark shapes like amoebae moving downwards under sloping slabs of ice.

Two days later I went up Grey Friar from Seathwaite Tarn. Before long I was above the clouds, which doesn't happen very often because I don't usually go up in the mist. I could see the tops of Caw and the Black Combe range but I couldn't see Stickle Pike because it wasn't high enough. When I got higher, I could see the top of the cloud extending right across the Irish Sea with Ingleborough and the highest peaks of Snowdonia sticking out of it. On the way down I saw what looked like masses of white waterfalls at the top of the cloud layer. It must have been some sort of mirage.

Although my name appears on the cover, all the changes you see in Books 5, 6 and 7 were made by Kate Cave. All I did was to provide the pencil drawings on which her work was based. She is also responsible for some of the layout. On High Pike 12 in Book 5, for example, I just typed out the text and asked if she could get it to fit by sacrificing the illustration in the bottom left-hand corner. Then she did the rest.

One day the books will need revising again. Perhaps there is a young person reading this who will take up the challenge.

Article published in the Wainwright Society magazine *Footsteps* in 2014

In 2009 I wrote an article for this magazine about my revision of the seven Lakeland guides. Since then I have been working on the revision of *A Coast to Coast Walk*, *The Outlying Fells of Lakeland*, *Pennine Way Companion*, *Walks in*

Limestone Country and *Walks on the Howgill Fells*. This article continues the story where the other one left off.

For ten years and six months, between 2003 and 2013, I devoted my life to this work, and I only just managed to finish it before I became too old to climb mountains. John Pulford must surely have noticed how quickly he caught me up and how quickly he left me behind when I met him in the Howgill Fells. If I hadn't dropped all other activities the work would never have been completed.

All the time I was working on the seven Lakeland guides I never saw an adder, but in the outlying fells I saw two, one on Bigland Barrow and the other on Walna Scar. On 23rd March 2011, as I was passing the hide at Low Birk Hatt (*Pennine Way Companion*, page 79) I saw five toads, and I mentioned them in the record book in the hide. I didn't see a newt on any of my walks until 7th August 2013, when I had finished the twelve volumes and was checking the starts of the Lakeland paths. It was on the slopes of Harter Fell, near the top of Hardknott Pass, and nowhere near any water.

The most remarkable sighting from this period was not in the mountains but fifty yards from my home in Kendal, when I saw a family of otters in the River Kent. Two things surprised me about them. One was that they were active in the middle of the day, and the other was that they behaved quite naturally, ignoring all the people who were watching them. I have seen foxes in the middle of the day, but only in very remote places, and I have only seen badgers very early in the morning before it gets light.

On 19th November 2009 I noticed that the River Kent was exceptionally high and I later learnt that twelve inches of rain had been recorded at Seathwaite that day in 24 hours, beating the record set up in Dorset in 1955. I went back there later and couldn't see any signs of flooding at Seathwaite, but I could at Lanthwaite Green, where the two footbridges and the remains of the weir had all been swept away. It occurs to me that the only reason that Seathwaite holds the record is that that is where the rain gauge happens to be.

I remember seeing in one of Wainwright's Lakeland sketchbooks people walking on the ice at Derwent Water and never thought I would live to see it, but I saw it twice, on 9th January 2010 and again on 22nd December of the same year. On both occasions Windermere was completely free of ice.

People sometimes write that I set off at the same time each day, but that is not true. I time my departure so that I start walking just as it gets light, and that varies from 4.00am in June to 8.00am in December. The earliest I left home was 1.30am on July 3rd 2010 when I was working in the Cheviots. I think that my longest day was when I left home at 4.00am, walked from Edale to Kinder Scout and back and got home at 9.00pm. The longest wasted journey I had was on 19th June 2010, when I reached the summit of the Cheviot from the east and had to turn back because my hands were frozen. It hadn't occurred to me that I would need gloves in June.

When I read on page 267 of the *Outlying Fells* that sheep could be trapped by their horns in a wire-mesh fence I thought that this was most unlikely, but near Glendue Burn on the Pennine Way (page 45) I encountered a sheep in exactly that predicament and was able to extricate it. This was not easy, and the sheep didn't seem to realise that I was trying to help. The same day I stopped to talk to the poet Colin Simms, who was sitting beside the lane above Garrigill with his binoculars and writing poetry. Another person I stopped to talk to was John Morrison. He was working on a book about the Pennine Way when I was working on the *Coast to Coast Walk* and we met where the two paths crossed.

As in the case of Books 5, 6 and 7 of the Lakeland guides, the alterations to *A Coast to Coast Walk*, *The Outlying Fells of Lakeland* and *Pennine Way Companion* were made by Kate Cave using a computer in the Frances Lincoln office. For *Walks in Limestone Country* and *Walks on the Howgill Fells* I made the alterations myself using a computer provided by the publishers. I would never have mastered it if it hadn't been for the help given to me by Dan Hodge, but when I did master it I was astonished at how much easier it was than making the alterations in pen and ink. What impressed me most was how much the image can be enlarged on the screen. If I had wanted to I could have made a full stop as big as a saucer.

On 16th November 2013 I asked the publishers to find a successor, and five days later I heard that Clive Hutchby, the author of the Wainwright Companion, would be taking over from me. Studying his book convinces me that nobody is better qualified to continue the work.

In 2015 the twenty-four-hour rainfall record was beaten again in the Lake District, and the River Kent was two and a half feet higher than it was in 2009.

In the introductions to the Lakeland guides, I mentioned the advantages I had over Wainwright. I had a car, for example; I had satellite navigation equipment, and I didn't have to go to work. What I forgot to mention was that by the time I was working there were accurate weather forecasts. As recently as 1992 I wrote in my diary that life would be a lot easier if it were possible to predict the weather. By 2003 I had discovered a telephone service called the Lake District Weather Line, which was so accurate I was hardly ever caught out by the rain. When it came to the Coast to Coast Walk the

Weather Line was no help because the weather in the North York Moors could be quite different from that in the Lake District, but by the time I went there I had discovered an accurate Internet forecast that covered the whole country. Several times I set off from Kendal in rain, confident that it would clear up as I headed east, and it always did.

In the first paragraph of his 'personal notes' at the end of *The Central Fells*, Wainwright wrote that when he finished the Lakeland guides he would be too old to go over the ground again making such revisions as might be found to be necessary. When I started on the revision in 2003, I was actually older than he was at that time.

When I got the first batch of changes back from the publishers it was accompanied by a letter asking me to make a large number of alterations that spoiled my carefully planned layout. This made me feel like the man in the song who was digging a hole when a 'bloke in a bowler' asked him to 'dig it elsewhere'. Happily there came a time when the publishers learned to take the layout into consideration.

There was one place in Book One where I could not make sense of my survey, so I went back and did it again. I found that the line produced was the same shape as the original line but in a different place because the equipment had been adding or subtracting the same amount from all my readings. Since then I have always used at least two GPS units.

The most difficult problem was getting the text to fit the space. If the text was too long I could generally get it in by rephrasing it or omitting unimportant information, but if it was too short the problem sometimes seemed insurmountable. On Greyfriars 3 in Book 4, for example, Wainwright had written something that was no longer relevant and I just bodged it up. My editor at Frances Lincoln didn't like what I had written and replaced it with something that I didn't like. I felt that the only solution would be to fill the space with something that was completely unconnected with what was written before. I went to the public library and studied every book that might have something to say about the area. Eventually I found what I was looking for and filled the space with text that we were both happy with.

A similar problem arose with page 6 of *A Coast to Coast Walk*, but here I couldn't find any helpful information. I felt that I would never be able to fill the space, but I kept on thinking and thinking about the problem, and in the end I succeeded. On page 84 of *Pennine Way Companion* I was asked to replace three quarters of a page of obsolete text; for weeks I sent emails saying that I was working on it, but the white space was so enormous I didn't see how I could ever fill it. Now the page looks like any other and nobody would imagine the torment that went into it.

There was a tennis player called Jimmy Connors, and every time he played a good shot he gave a series of little jumps. I know exactly how he felt, because I felt the same whenever I got a paragraph to fit the space.

On 10th June 2006 I found the remains of a balloon a few yards from the summit of Coniston Old Man with a postcard attached asking for it to be returned to a school near Wigan, so I did so.

On page 59 of *A Coast to Coast Walk* there was a quarry that was still operating but had become very much larger, and I was able to show the extent of the quarry both in 1972 and in 2009. Remarkably, a similar opportunity presented itself on page 17 (1) of *Walks in Limestone Country*. At the foot of page Great Borne 4 in *The Western Fells* Wainwright mentioned that Croasdale was misspelt Crossdale on a signpost and I was able to say that it had been misspelt for more than forty years. Then a similar opportunity presented itself on page 31 (2) of *Walks in Limestone Country.*

When I started working on *The Outlying Fells of Lakeland* I bought a second-hand copy of the first edition. In it I found a press cutting in which somebody suggested that the route from Faulds Brow to Caldbeck should be diverted to visit the Howk. I thought that this was an excellent idea, and I featured this as an alternative route in the revised book.

Making changes using the computer was so easy that I was able to go through every page of *Walks on the Howgill Fells* (and, to a lesser extent, *Walks in Limestone Country*) cleaning up the places where the lines were too thick. To do this required so little thought that I was able to do it when I was too exhausted to make the more difficult changes. The improvement is obvious if you place the unrevised and revised pages side by side, but, so far as I know, nobody has noticed it.

Sales of revised Wainwright books up to August 2017:

(excluding those subsequently revised by Clive Hutchby)

Book 1 The Eastern Fells	27,776
Book 2 The Far Eastern Fells	18,900
Book 3 The Central Fell	21,416
Book 4 The Southern Fells	26,132
Book 5 The Northern Fells	17,758
Book 6 The North Western Fells	16,989
Book 7 The Western Fells	14,586
A Coast to Coast Walk	16,425
The Outlying Fells of Lakeland	6492
Pennine Way Companion	1459
Walks in Limestone Country	393
Walks on the Howgill Fells	360
The Best of Wainwright	6804
Wainwright TV Walks	5445
Total	180,935

When I thought the work was all over I was asked to make some alterations to *A Coast to Coast Walk* to reflect changes to the signposted route. I thought that in many cases the new route was not as satisfactory as the old one, but I am pleased to say that the very last change I made was an improvement: I described a new route that avoided the swamp on page 157.

I finished the work on the twelve pictorial guides on 15th July 2013, ten years and six weeks after I began. I continued working on the starts of the Lakeland paths until 11th December 2013, but the changes I made were never published. While I was revising the Wainwright books I felt, more than at any other time in my life, that I was a round peg in a round hole.

On 23rd December 2013 I took my car to the auction mart at Bamber Bridge near Preston. By this time the car was so old that all I received was £65. In ten years the car had only broken down twice, and on both occasions it happened within 200 yards of my home. When I bought a motor caravan in 1975 it broke down three times in the first thirty miles. When I bought another motor caravan in 1977, the throttle stuck open and the silencer went before I left the premises of the person I bought it from. And when I was trying out a kart with a view to buying it in 1965, the brake came off, the throttle slipped, the choke lever broke, the silencer became disconnected and the petrol tank broke loose, but fortunately all this happened before I agreed to buy it.

In 2005 I moved from my flat in Beast Banks to a small cottage at number 3, Yard 18, Kirkland in the old part of Kendal. In 2007 I moved to another small cottage at number 13, Longpool. Its best features were its lovely old doors with their long iron hinges. This was my only Kendal address that was not difficult to find. It was actually on the A6, which was the main road from London to Carlisle before the coming of the motorways. In 2008 I moved to a former council flat on the Kirkbarrow estate.

This was the least attractive of all my Kendal addresses, but after I had been there for eight years I realised that how long I was allowed to stay in a place was far more important than what it looks like.

In my flat in Beast Banks I encountered a strange blob that turned into powder when I touched it, and I wondered if it was a slime mould. In my flat in Anchorite Place I found something similar, and this time I was able to identify it with certainty because an identical one was illustrated on the Internet.

Family tree

In March 2007 I tried to construct a Jesty family tree using the Internet but without success. In October of the same year I received an incredibly detailed and well-designed family tree from a distant relative. There were 800 names in it, but my own branch was missing. I sent an email to Professor Jolyon Jesty, who compiled the tree, adding the missing information, which was finally incorporated in 2013. This story was similar to that of the Old Buckwellians (the society of former pupils of Buckhurst Hill County High School). I tried to contact them without success in 1993, and then in 2002 I found out that they were trying to contact me.

I was disappointed to learn that I was not descended from Benjamin Jesty the smallpox pioneer as I had always believed, but I was pleased to learn that I was descended from a succession of eighteenth-century farmers from the Dorset villages of Yetminster, Chetnole and Leigh. These three villages were the subject of a television programme that was so good that I would have kept selections from it even if there hadn't been a family connection.

On 11th January 2009 Jonathan de Ferranti made it possible for people to view my panoramas on the internet at: www.viewfinderpanoramas.org/panoramas/ChrisJestyPanoramas.html.

It is surprising that he was able to do this, because some of the panoramas are too big even for an A3 scanner. At first it took ten minutes to get a panorama on the screen, but later I could do this instantaneously, I also learned how to enlarge the image so that I could read the small lettering, and to move from one part of the image to another.

One of the first things I did when I finished working on the Wainwright books was to sort out my possessions. Among the things I threw away were ninety maps, twenty-five pens, nineteen pencils and eleven rolls of adhesive tape. My next task was to create my own website. This included scans of the pages of my five books and the video of my journey to Africa in 1995. It was explained to me that I would have to provide a long thin photograph for the site, and I found one of Harrison Stickle from Scafell Pike that was ideal.

One of the most interesting emails I received through my website came from Simon Burnill. He claimed that the widest-ranging view in Britain was from the Merrick in southern Scotland, because it extended from Snowdon in the south to Ben More on Mull in the north, and he wanted to know whether I agreed with him. I replied that I had never considered the question before, but now that I had done so I had come to the conclusion that it was very unlikely that a greater example would ever be found.

In 2012 I was asked to contribute to a book about John Nicoll, the managing director of Frances Lincoln, but I never heard any more about it. Here is my contribution:

> In 1991 I prepared revised editions of the first two volumes of Wainwright's Lakeland guides, but I couldn't get anyone to take an interest in them. I felt that what I needed was a person who appreciated the value of what I was doing and could promote my ideas. Twelve years later, in 2003, that person finally turned up: it was John Nicoll.

Scrap books

Since 1979 I have added items to my scrapbooks as soon as they become available.

Volume 15 includes selected rough drafts of fifteen unpublished panoramas and YHA membership cards with 128 stamps on from 1969 onwards.

Volume 25 consists of forty-six pages of photographs taken between 1981 and 1985.

Volume 28 includes press reviews for *East Anglian Town Trails* and eight pages of revision notes for the

Wainwright books produced as a sample in 1988.

Volume 30 consists of forty-two pages of photographs, including those taken in Switzerland in 1985. My favourite photograph from this volume is that of an old door in the village of Symondsbury near Bridport.

Volume 32 includes the map I produced for *Wainwright's Favourite Lakeland Mountains* and the three maps I produced for *Walking the Peak and Pennines* by Mike Harding.

Volume 33 includes photographs of Robin Hood's Bay and Chapel Close.

Volume 35 includes photographs from my flats in Chapel Close and Beast Banks.

Volume 36 includes the Jesty family tree and various press cuttings about my work on the Wainwright books.

By 2014 the more interesting pages of my scrapbooks had been scanned because by this time there was much more room on the discs. When I first had this idea I could only get one page on a disc. In 2014 I got over 700 pages onto a storage device that is easy to copy and small enough to go into a purse. This way the contents of the books may be expected to survive much longer than the books themselves would have done.

From 1948 until 1984 my scrapbooks were my most treasured possessions. Then their place was taken by my collection of scenes from television.

On 3rd March 2014 I donated a computer disc containing my diary and the best of my writings to the Great Diary

Project in the hope that they will last forever. At this time my diary was 380,000 words long. On 29th March, I went to the Wainwright Society AGM in Staveley village hall, where the chairman, Eric Robson, called me to the front and presented me with an inscribed tankard for my work on the Wainwright books. This I regard as the crowning achievement of my life. It came as a pleasant surprise, and the moment was captured in a photograph taken by the editor of *Footsteps*, David Johnson.

Lightning Source UK Ltd.
Milton Keynes UK
UKHW02f1346140618

324203UK00001B/1/P